HUMAN
WISDOM OF LOVE AND SCIENCE

HUMAN
WISDOM OF LOVE AND SCIENCE

MUSTAFA PAYESIZ

978-1-80541-505-3 (paperback)
978-1-80541-504-6 (eBook)

CONTENTS

PREFACE (1)

If you watch television today, you owe it to the invention of electricity, which was invented before television. For instance, it is impossible to create an order sequence, such as "Let the television be invented first, then we'll look into electricity." However, in our daily lives, we unconsciously make many mistakes that undermine the importance of such an order. These errors are due to the confusion of the cause-effect sequence in our consciousness, and the fact that we often treat the results as a cause and ignore the real cause. We will examine and see the contradictions of many beliefs that have come to light, which arise from this order, within the topics we will cover.

If we look at things from the perspective of science and technology, we are much more advanced today than in the past. For example, whilst electricity was used only in lighting in the past, today it is present in almost every aspect of our lives. Although science and technology entered our lives with this momentum and surrounded us, we could not break the patterns of thousands of years and kept going around in a circle when it came to faith and philosophy, and we were imprisoned in these narrow patterns. On the one hand, we have amplified and progressed the electrical knowledge that Tesla and Edison left us, on the other hand, even today, we have not been able to understand Hallâc-ı Mansûr and

Seyyid Nesîmî. We have not understood the light they shed on consciousness and belief. As a result, voids like black holes have formed in our spiritual heartland and we have fallen into these voids.

The statements that are presented to people as 'Beliefs', are not factual. They are simply beliefs. They do not convince anyone. They bind and strangle mankind like a straight-jacket that is forced upon them. Although the origins of beliefs have not yet been solved from past to present, they should be put in the right place and clarified today. This can be done by explaining 'Belief' in a scientific manner.

As non-scientific belief definitions will not be accurate, these definitions will remain as a teaching fixed in the perception of people who do not question the universe and human reality. The value of the people who synthesised faith and the reality of the universe in the past is more clearly understood today.

If scientists such as Einstein and Newton had perceived their scientific work as "interfering in God's work" and had not brought the mind to the fore, many things that were done would probably not have been done today. On the other hand, if Hallâc-ı Mansûr had not been hanged a thousand years ago for being rational, if Seyyid Nesîmî had not been flayed five hundred years ago, and if humanity had been able to choose to be rational, it is sure that today there would be no hunger, global warming, and wars today.

Now, each person who lives on Earth should understand that there is no option other than being a rationalist.

Otherwise, it is very clear that there is no future for humanity.

PREFACE (2)

I will tell you two stories about how we think of events and evaluate them. These stories, which enable us to question the extent to which our own evaluation and perception are accurate, and show how our perceptions can mislead us, serve as an example illustrating that we should look at events from many perspectives to comprehend the truths.

Many years ago, humorous stories were published in the middle pages of a humour magazine. I read a humour story in an issue of the magazine called "The Diary of a Mad Person". In summary, this story explained that the character was locked up in a psychiatric hospital and imprisoned within four walls. In his own words, the story explained the immediate escape of the character from hospital, and the 'naughtiness' he was involved in within this period while 'smart-alecks'" thought that they had locked him up. The interesting aspect of the story is that this so-called "escape from hospital" was not an escape in reality, instead, it was actually moving away from there with his mind or consciousness while his body remained in the hospital. In other words, the story expressed the character's mental escape rather than physical escape from the hospital, and explained the naughtiness he did.

As a matter of fact, we all think of, and do, the same things because our consciousness is not a phenomenon confined to our body. In short, we are all naughty and "mad".

What I was told many years ago when I first started my working life was that I should know I did not have the chance to please and convince everybody at the same time and I should do my work in accordance with this.

In fact, this was almost a warning for people to put their expectations to one side and do the work in compliance with their own nature. The reason for this was shown with the "donkey and passengers" example, which we all know.

In this given example, a man and woman were walking in the countryside with a donkey, and portrays the following observations of different people's perspectives of these scenarios.

If the man got on the donkey, his action suggested that he was disrespectful and rude towards the woman, if he decided to be the one on the donkey it was because he did not care about the woman.

If the woman got on the donkey, this scenario suggested that the man let the woman on the donkey because he was more passive and less capable than the woman.

If neither the woman nor the man got on the donkey, this scenario suggested that the woman and man were both fools.

And finally, if both the woman and the man got on the donkey, this scenario suggested that neither of them felt pity for the donkey because they were unscrupulous and careless.

As can be seen, whatever the option is, people want to define the events with their own perceptions, independently of the truth of the matter. When we realise this truth, we also comprehend the truth that our perception may not always be correct. I am writing this because I know that it is difficult to go beyond people's normal or traditional thoughts. I also know that people will read this book with their own views and try to understand the expressions through their own viewpoint. Therefore, I would like you to know that the topics explained here are dealt with in two perspectives. While, on one hand, the topics are explained objectively from a scientific perspective and on the other hand, dealt within the framework of people's acceptance and belief systems. As a result, whilst reading this book, some parts may sound very familiar, others may sound incomprehensible and unnecessarily repetitive. If you feel this way, please remember this preface before making a judgement and continue to read without making any preconceptions. For instance, think that your own opinion and judgement may not always be realistic. Question the probability that many things of which you are actually very sure about aren't always true in reality. You will realise many truths about humanity and the universe when you are not prejudiced whilst reading this book.

I wish I could define and explain the topics using plain language. However, as you can appreciate, the matters and topics will get complicated when you try to explain the functioning laws of the universe through events. Therefore, you will encounter many definitions that have different patterns and functions in almost every aspect regarding the laws of the universe. When you find expressions that seem repetitive to you, please understand it is done with intent, so as to fully explain the concept in its entirety and to communicate an emphasis on a particular topic.

PREFACE (3)

The topics that I will explain are actually the roadmap of ancient teaching. This map includes the present-day narration and synthesis of the teaching of existence and humanity, which are based on rationalism and science and have been ongoing for thousands of years. This is the rational analysis of this teaching, which is based on "Vahdet-i Vücûd" and "Enel Hak", about existence and humankind.

If we call this road "the road to the truth", we can say that this book is the reopening of a case that has been tried for thousands of years and is now reignited with new evidence. In our present day, you are the jury of this case.

However, our aim will not be to convince you. We do not aim to question people's beliefs or consciousness. Here, the aim is that you face your opinions and your own consciousness for justice and fairness to be done. The intention is to be able to see the fairness of people's judgments against others. Perhaps, this is an opportunity given to you so that you can learn who you are. In the end, there will not be a good or bad definition of the destination where you will arrive in our perspective. However, you will define yourself and this is our responsibility for humanity.

INTRODUCTION

I don't think it is incorrect to call the era we live in the information era. We live in a period when access to all the information compiled from the beginning of time until today is at our fingertips – just by clicking on a single button. However, here, the main problem is the possibility of the information we access being true or false. This is because we should first know what correct information is in order to determine whether the information is true or false. Otherwise, we can believe that all information we obtain is true. For the information that we say "it is true" to be true, it should also need to be verified by others. The only information that can be absolutely proven and verified to be true is science. This is because scientific information is not subject to any process due to its characteristic of being verifiable by everyone in all circumstances. We can believe in such verifiable information with peace of mind and say that "it is true". If you cannot verify this information, then it is very natural that there is doubt, and existence of such doubt is an indicator of the fact that truth is deemed important. Hence, it is not correct that people could be suspicious about verified facts because realism is limited to being either true or false and is not relative.

Today, people produce information that mainly has two aims. The first is the information aimed at really contributing to, and improving, humanity. The other is the information aimed at using people's ignorance for one's own interests or purposes. Today, unfortunately, we encounter such information pollution very frequently. Everyone who has hearsay information thinks that they are scientists. Many things can be said about this subject; however, it would be useful to keep in mind the words of Socrates, "All I know is that I know nothing".

In addition to today's information pollution, we also have information pollution from the past; and we experience the most serious problems with this incorrect information. This is the information that has been ongoing for thousands of years and is almost ingrained in our genes. This information, which has been accepted as true for thousands of years, is the information of faith, science, philosophy, and history. Some of this information is true and some of it is false. As we were born in this environment of information, we have been equipped with wrong or incomplete information since the early years of our childhood. If you look at the problems that we experience today, you will see the negative reflections of this wrong and incomplete information on our lives in the foundation of these problems. Today, sorting out this information and accessing true information has become almost obligatory. For example, if I said that the Earth is not revolving, I suppose no one would take it seriously. However, unfortunately, there is a presence of people who claim that the Earth is, in fact, not revolving, even today, which is a grievous situation for humanity. Should we see things with the logic of "Ignorance is bliss" and "If a man is happy in his situation, there is no problem"? – or should we think that "We should do something and find a way to tell that person the truth"? If ignorance were bliss, we would have to close all schools; because ignorance is not bliss, but people deceiving themselves and resisting change. The system operating in the universe is that everything changes and transforms. Resisting this change is resisting the laws of nature. We don't have an option to resist, because every structure that does not act appropriately to change is destroyed by the operating system. There are also people that want to look at the operating system of the universe from their own window. For example, those people may attribute their own insincerity to the system saying that "There exists a running system and we are keeping up with it." The argument of "The fact that we also do injustice and are selfish in order to survive is something that the system imposes on us. So, we act appropriately to the system and protect ourselves by doing so. Thus, we are innocent!" is not sincere. If this were true, we would not have humanistic and conscientious traits and the option to have such traits. This is because if the two options are good and bad, selecting the one that serves our purpose and defending it by saying that "It is the requirement of the system", is not the requirement of the system, it is our manipulation of the purpose.

As we understand from this example, in addition to whether the information is true or false, people's intention and sincerity in using this information is also as important as the information itself. The fact that people act insincerely is somehow related to the extent to which the information is objective or relative. It is not possible that you insincerely interpret scientific information in your own way. However, it is very easy for you to do that through the arguments of beliefs, and in this case, you can encounter thousands of conflicting comments.

Situations like these show how really necessary it is for knowledge to be scientific. For now, it is not right to assume that it is natural to experience these things because human consciousness does not have the capability of directly obtaining true information. In fact, it is almost an irresponsibility to remain unresponsive to it.

The fact that people's information increases and evolves into a healthy structure occurs within a certain period. However, it is inevitable that filters exist through which we will rapidly eliminate false information. These filters are scientific queries and scientific data.

1
CONSCIOUSNESS

In order to understand the subjects that we will discuss, first we should understand what our comprehension, interpretation, decision-making, and preference consciousnesses mean, how they are formed, and how they operate.

Consciousness is the main subject of philosophy, science, and belief systems and is a system that has been operating since the moment we came into existence. Even if we think that we have free will and the ability to think independently, this is not completely true. Consciousness depends on certain parameters and the operating laws of the universe. At this point, consciousness is universal and is not a system that operates arbitrarily.

So, now we have ascertained that consciousness is universal and depends on the operation of the universe, then we should first try to understand the formation and operation of our consciousness. If we recognise and understand the active parameters in our own consciousness and follow the operation of consciousness together, then it will be easier to understand consciousness itself. Once we understand what consciousness is, we will have solved many problems automatically.

Picture, if you will, that you are on top of a hill. Zoom in on yourself on a satellite in the depth of the universe with a satellite remote control in your hand and look at yourself on the hill. Then slowly zoom out. You will notice that you will become smaller and look like a dot, and then the world will become smaller and also look like a dot, and finally, the solar system will become smaller and look like a dot; and when you disappear and become invisible, will you think that you really have become smaller and disappeared or will you feel that nothing has changed on that hill? In fact, you are in a dimension in your own objectivity, but at the same time, you are as small as nothing in the space-time dimension. In other words, you are doing and living this with your consciousness in your brain. You are in the exact moment when you are as small as infinity, and at the same time, you are the space-time dimension itself.

As consciousness, humans are the evolution of "energy" and the place you are looking around is the space-time dimension. The space-time layers [1] are the evolutionary process of energy. We can consider this as the process of understanding the consciousness of the "consciousness". In other words, we can define it as the process of understanding the consciousness of the "consciousness" that brings the universe into existence. The consciousness that creates the universe or brings it into existence is the same consciousness that is in the universe itself and is everywhere. In the universe in which we live, what is active in our consciousness is the structure of matter and energy and our consciousness has a passive nature, which is the product of this matter and energy conversions. If our consciousness was active, it would have the chance to experience itself and we would be able to control the universal laws with it; for example, we could eliminate gravity and make a piece of stone that we throw on the ground take wings and fly instead of falling to

1 This indicates the process of change from the Big Bang until today and the process that will pass until the other transformation of the universe after that.

the ground. However, we all know that we cannot know what the consciousness of our own consciousness is.

In addition, if existence was not under the control of matter and the laws of energy, our consciousness would not already have content integrity. Conflicts like the fact that good and bad occur at the same time, or that an object falls downwards and upwards at the same time could be experienced, or something would attempt to happen in this way because we wish it, and things that are difficult to define would happen.

For all these reasons, human consciousness is not active, but passive, and existence is controlled by universal laws. The fact that consciousness experiences itself in the space-time dimension (matter-energy), this is what we feel as emotions and thoughts. Consciousness works within an eternal probability range. Mind, on the other hand, is limited and realistic and filters the probabilities that do not comply with the universal laws.

Let's briefly define:

- **Mind** is the balance and attachment of our active and passive consciousness.
- **Passive consciousness** is the trait of breaking the rules and believing that everything can be possible and that a person did or will do everything by themselves.
- **Active consciousness,** on the other hand, is the struggle to comprehend that rules and universal laws exist and to know their limits.

Because consciousness is passive in the system operating in the universe, domination of **rationalism** in our lives is the only essential way. This is because balancing what is rational and what is imaginary to prevent all negative events is only possible with rationalism. We will explain what these mean throughout the chapters. However, because the structure and operation of consciousness is a technical subject, it may be incomprehensible for the reader at first glance. If there are subjects that cannot be understood when you first read about them, you will find meaning in the following chapters and then you will have the opportunity to understand the subjects better. I expect your understanding on this matter.

NOTE: What we understand when consciousness is in question actually includes many phenomena such as comprehension, the ability to think, the ability to apprehend, the ability to understand, the ability to know, the ability to learn, and the ability to compare.

I request that you evaluate the meaning of the word "consciousness" as we use it throughout the chapters, as appropriate to each subject.

THE PARAMETERS THAT CREATE CONSCIOUSNESS

The Law Of Necessity

The law of necessity is the main law and principle in the existence and operation of the universe. Why is the sum of the interior angles of a triangle 180 degrees, or why is the division of the perimeter of a circle by its diameter a constant number (pi)? The universal constants for which you cannot find an answer when you ask the question "why" for hundreds of topics like this are addressed within the scope of the law of necessity. These constants have their own causalities and they are the reasons that none of us can know what they are.

It is impossible for the universe to exist and operate without constant and universal laws like this. What creates our consciousness, which questions and seeks to answer this, is already these laws. In other words, we do not have the chance to understand the causality of the laws that create the causality of our own consciousness. We cannot already exist, think, and interpret without these laws.

The law of necessity is based on the principle and fact that "**singularity**" does not, and cannot, exist. This is because singularity means nothing exists other than singularity. In other words, it means no structure that will create, know, and understand the singularity exists other than that singularity itself. Yet, there should be at least two structures – **defining** and **defined** – for a meaning to exist. Without another structure (person), a structure (person) cannot self-define truth and meaning. For something to have a meaning, there should be another structure (person) who can understand and define the truth and basis of meaning besides the structure (person) who has expressed the meaning.

The requirement of the existence of this structure with at least two different components (defining-defined) is called the law of symmetry. One of these two components is a material, energy-oriented or objective structure, and the other component is the passive quantitative structure that is formed in the movement of this structure, and interprets it. We can call it the dimension of consciousness. If we reduce these two components to the quantum level and call the matter and energy structure the information dimension, the dimension that is formed in return for the movement of this information dimension will be the meaning dimension (the consciousness dimension). The structure that we call energy is actually information and potentially carries the consciousness within. In other words, energy carries its own principles and laws and its own operation information within. The combination of the meaning and information dimensions is the cosmos dimension that covers everything. There is no universal dimension and reality other than the cosmos dimension. These structures cannot be separated and thought to be different from each other. The combination of these two structures potentially carries the possibility of the existence of everything within itself. What determines the feasibility of everything that is formed in the universe, is the laws and principles of the universe. In other words, it is universal laws that determine which one of the potentially possible formations will exist. These are the laws of necessity and the universal constants. The things that enable the administration of the system that operates at the meaning level (our consciousness) are these laws themselves and their principles. **We can also define them as the laws of necessity and the principles of causality, or characterise them as structural and functional, or active and passive**. We define the operation of these laws as movement (active and passive operation). A passive meaning (consciousness) dimension is formed in the movement in a main energy structure (information). Without movement, the existence and meaning of these structures would not be formed and revealed. With the movement of these structures, the existence and meaning dimensions of these structures are also formed. With the beginning of movement, the phenomena that we know such as existence, time, information, meaning, mathematics, and consciousness find meaning and become comprehensible and understood. Essentially, these are inseparable and intertwined structures – but we separated them to correctly explain the events. This is because if we do not make this separation, a possibility appears for us to confuse the qualitative and quantitative characteristics and make mistakes. For example, if you try to measure kilogram and kilocalorie with the same scale, you will find this impossible because these are structures with different characteristics. Therefore, we should make the necessary separation and definition considering this in order to make our definitions correctly. Because of this requirement, you make a mistake if you try to explain the laws of necessity with the principles of causality. You encounter a meaningless situation – just like trying to weigh heat in a scale – you cannot prioritise a structure that is a product as the producing element and ignore the real producer. For example, you cannot prioritise the existence of a water molecule formed of oxygen and hydrogen (H_2O) as the source structure that creates the "hydrogen and oxygen" elements. This is because water is the product that results from these two components and cannot create the structure that creates it. In other words, you can produce hydrogen and oxygen in the water (H_2O) molecule but you cannot say that water has brought them into existence. This is because oxygen and hydrogen already existed before the first water molecule, and water was formed after them. You may think that not taking this order into consideration will be a great and obvious mistake. However, I want you to know that we make thousands of mistakes like this unconsciously. For example, seeking an answer for a structural phenomenon with the question "Why does it exist?" is a meaningless situation. This is because the question "why" is valid only in the case of the existence of an existing phenomenon. A structural phenomenon either exists or does not exist, and the question "why" is not a phenomenon that can be interpreted. Similarly, we could not ask the question "why" if we did not exist. This is because our existence is necessary for us to be able to ask this question. In other words, there is an order here. The necessity comes before the consciousness that can ask the question "why". This necessity that the structural phenomenon should exist before consciousness itself is also a law of necessity and comes before the question "why". In other words, "necessity" is **active** and "causality" is its **passive** form. The necessity-causality relationship is also in question within the framework of the cause-effect relationship. If you think without taking this situation into consideration, you can miss out on many things and make mistakes.

"**Thinking by prioritising causality is similar to the mistake that we ourselves wanted to exist, we prepared the circumstances to create ourselves, and we brought ourselves into existence**." However, no formation can exist before the structure that creates it and the structure that creates it. For example, you could not have brought your parents into existence in order to be born. Thus, the active and passive operation is **extremely** important. At this point, you are not the **active** creatures that bring your parents into existence; you are the **passive** creatures that are brought into existence by them. You cannot be the **active** creatures that bring them together to create your own existence. Thus, you cannot define your own passiveness as activeness, and similarly, you also cannot bring **causality** before **necessity**. Of course the basis of science is questionable; however, it is also essential to make realistic queries. Technically, if we cannot make a correct query, it is inevitable that we make mistakes. We make thousands of mistakes in life without realising. We will increase these examples by addressing many of them throughout the chapters.

The law of necessity is the most basic law that also includes the consciousness dimension in addition to the space-time dimension. What we call consciousness is a passive comprehension dimension that is formed by the joint and intersection of many parameters of the "moment". The thing that makes this comprehension meaningful and understandable is the fact that there are operating universal laws and that they are operational. For example, if the conceptual contrast of hot and cold did not exist, we could not define heat and no concept could be formed about heat and temperature in our consciousness. In other words, everything should have a contrast or complement for our consciousness to be formed. This necessity for a contrast or difference is called **the law of symmetry**. Then, there should be a difference of contrast or comparison and we should understand them so that we can find something meaningful. Presence of this interpretation requires the existence of a **consciousness of causality** and a law of **necessity** which creates that causality. In other words, if a magnetism is formed in the Earth's poles, this requires the facts that the Earth exists and revolves. This is because otherwise, magnetism would not have been formed. This is the case for the matter and energy dimension. It is also the case for consciousness. The fact that matter has the micro and macro dimensions depends on this law of necessity. The separating line between these two dimensions is the **plane of symmetry** (separation surface).

Every formation in the universe has symmetry. This plane (area) of symmetry is also the area of **activeness-passiveness** and the reference point of information and symmetry. Without the area or plane of symmetry, our consciousness and meaning would not already be formed. This is because a comparison and meaning awareness could not be formed as there was no symmetry contrast. The thing that makes us different and special in the world we live in is that we have this comparison and conscious awareness, and that we interpret and question the universe's operation. All these concepts depend on each other and cannot be separated from each other. As we continue, we will portray how these concepts fit together, and their relationships with each other will be understood.

Most people have questioned why they exist and the aim of their existence. Even questioning this, is a result of the operating universal laws. Beliefs define the reason for this with other arguments in their way. However, when we understand what the source of the thing we call consciousness or belief depends on, or does not depend on, or when we learn what can be possible, and what is impossible in life, we prevent the fact that people impose their own unfounded opinions as "true information" and abuse our sincerity. Thus, future generations will also be freed of these negative structures and there will be no waste of time for humanity.

First of all, we should know that our consciousness is not a structure that is specifically sent to humans and living creatures from somewhere and that is recorded. For example, scientists cloned animals like sheep and horses and these creatures came to life. So, did people force "God" to give these creatures a soul and life by this cloning? In other words, did "God" have to give a soul and life to these creatures that people cloned? We will understand the answers to questions like this, which we all consider to be true or false, together.

First, if we are living and breathing now, then we can say that there cannot be something that can be deemed "absolute" and a "singularity". This is because for an existence to be present, the structure that will create this existence should be transformed or triggered by a factor other than itself. **In other words, an object cannot transform and create its own objectivity by itself.** It is absolutely necessary that a different structure exists in that objectivity, and that this structure transforms that objectivity. This is just like the situation where gelatine dynamite needs a fuse to explode. This means that the structure that existed before the Big Bang must have had at least two components. This situation requires the existence of both the law of **necessity** and the law of **symmetry**. This is because the Big Bang and existence could not have occurred without these laws. If the universe exists as a requirement of the existence of these laws, then a structure that corresponds to the total quantity of matter and energy existing in the universe today must have existed before the Big Bang. That exact "moment" of explosion is the point of symmetry. In other words, this "moment" is the transition point between the structure called "nothing" and existence, the transformation point between the periods before and after the Big Bang, or the initial moment of the transition from one form to another. Similarly, if we have consciousness today, this requires the existence of a consciousness in the structure before the Big Bang. This is because existence cannot occur from a structure that does not exist (see the first principle of thermodynamics). However, the existence of a consciousness before existence does not mean a consciousness defined by a belief system, and is not the way the universe is created to think. This consciousness has been transformed from the structure before the Big Bang to the structure after the Big Bang. This consciousness is already everywhere in the universe and, living or nonliving; everything has this consciousness. However, this consciousness is not limited to the consciousness in our perception. Because everything's consciousness depends on its own objectivity, we know that every formation has a consciousness even if we do not understand it. For example, gravity acts like the consciousness of water while streams are moving – or we can also address the quantum operation in the micro dimension of the universe as one consciousness of the Creator. We can also consider the transformation of a piece of stone into soil over time as consciousness. These laws operate like they are the consciousness of the events and formations in the universe. We have not been able to fully understand and solve this operation. However, we know that there is a necessity in this operation, no matter what. For example, we know that if there is mass, this mass cannot resist the force of gravity. This is because the existence of mass requires that it abides by gravity. This is an inevitable situation. In other words, the existence of mass does not offer the option to resist gravity. Absence of such an option is the **law of necessity** itself. Everything in the universe acts according to the laws of necessity. The fact that we question the events that occurred according to the law of necessity is included within the scope of the **principle of causality. Thus, existence of a formation requires the existence of a necessity and causality.**

On the other hand, our causality consciousness has a passive nature because it is a structure that emerged later. In other words, we are the results of the process of existence and the progress of the universe and hence, are regarded as passive creatures because we were formed later. Coincidentally, we are also active creatures, for the future, because what we will do in the future depends on today's structure. In short, us humans are actually both active and passive creatures because we live as of the "moment". We are regarded as **passive** creatures according to the past and **active** creatures according to the future.

We cannot know the structure of consciousness before the Big Bang; however, we cannot address what is called consciousness in the universe we live in as a structure that independently works in matter and energy, and that does not belong to this universe. Hence, if there is a creator consciousness, this consciousness is already with us and the existence of another consciousness in a different place from us (cosmos), except for our own consciousness, is out of the question. In other words, if there is no objectivity; if there is no existence, consciousness cannot exist either (see the law of necessity).

Even if you accept that there is consciousness, this consciousness cannot interpret and experience itself without an existence (see the singularity of consciousness). Therefore, in the case that there is either **consciousness** or an **existence**, the existence of the other is necessary. The availability of both is essential. This means the existence of our consciousness requires the existence of our matter structure. Similarly, the existence of matter requires that it has a consciousness. However, we ignore non-living things because we do not understand their consciousness.

Our experiences, emotions, and senses belong to ourselves, and are part of the experiences of the collaborative universal consciousness. This means while we were a part of this consciousness before the Big Bang, now we are a part of the universal consciousness and the Creator in terms of both our matter structure and our consciousness. This is the consciousness which is within us all and to which we calibrate ourselves, for example, this is what makes us feel guilt when we hurt another living creature; makes us feel uncomfortable when we lie – and is something everyone is already aware of. We feel these experiences – their meanings, their good or bad references – from that consciousness already within.

The Law Of Active-Passive

The concepts of active and passive are the operations that represent a movement, change, transformation, formation, or reflection. When a guitar string vibrates, it generates a sound wave. The guitar string is a structural phenomenon and represents an active structure. The sound wave formed by the vibration of the string, on the other hand, is a passive structure that the active structure produces or generates. For instance, while the mass existence of the Earth is a structural phenomenon and an active structure, the magnetism formed in its poles when the Earth revolves is a passive structure that the Earth generates. The fact that seas and oceans fluctuate as the moon rotates around the Earth is also a passive structure. The fuse of a kerosene lamp has an active structure, and the light and heat formed when the fuse is lit is a passive structure. A radioactive element has an active structure, and the process of losing mass and energy by radiating is an active-passive structure. The universe itself is a structural phenomenon that has continued by expanding and progressing within itself since the Big Bang until present day. The movement between a moment before and a moment after in this structure is ongoing, and continuous. If we define a moment before as active, the structure of a moment after is the passive form of the structure of the moment before, because a moment after will have altered. This situation operates every moment as active-passive. In other words, as long as there is movement in a phenomenon, that phenomenon is both active and passive. In this operation, we should not confuse the objective structures and non-objective passive structures or the theoretical structures. In mathematics, the sum of the structural numbers that we know is 0.1.2.3.4.5.6.7.8.9. and these numbers are the numbers that will remain constant until the end of the universe. These numbers have a natural theoretical structure, so we can't start creating new numbers in this universe, that would essentially be recreating mathematics. Creating a new number means that you create a new universe and operate this universe according to the new number that you have added. Although these numbers are conceptually constant and invariant, we create a number sequence that moves toward infinity with the combinations of these numbers (881, . . . 1240, . . . 3541333333333 . . .) and we are mistaken that numbers are infinite. However, the thing that moves toward infinity is not the numbers themselves, but their operational characteristics. What we do is to extend the combinations of these numbers, in other words, their passive structures, to infinity. The concept of limit in mathematics is an example of the conflict between objective structures and non-objective operation. If you stand at a distance of 5 metres from a wall and take a step in a way that every step you take is half of your previous step, mathematically, you cannot reach that wall. It is predicted that you cannot reach the wall even if you take steps forever. The conflict here is the fact that the operation of structural phenomenon and theoretical phenomenon are confused. This illusion is also effective in our correct understanding of quantum mechanics, and we confuse certain operations. Here, the attempt is to force the law and reality of the universe to comply with the conceptual assumption of mathematics. However, theoretically, you can divide an atom by infinity but this is rather impossible in practice. If you force an objective phenomenon into uncertainty or infinity, the universal laws do not allow this, and transforms the object not to uncertainty but to another phenomenon and continues its movement within its own laws.

This significance is the distinction between the universal laws and universal principles. Every law has a principle and every principle has an equivalent law. However, the point of distinction between them is whether they are qualitative or quantitative, in other words, being active and passive. Forcing a structural phenomenon into being quantitative would be a scenario similar to trying to hear only the sound of a violin in orchestral music. In other words, you cannot listen to the violin alone when all the sounds mix together while the orchestra is playing. All these operations are based on the balance of symmetry and this is a law of necessity. For example, if you have to balance a weighing scale's pans, when you put a weight on one pan of the scale, you should put an equal weight on the other pan. The operation in the universe is not stable (steady), it is in motion (moving). All these active and passive structures operate together, with all their combinations, simultaneously. The necessity of balance in this operation is a feature of the law of symmetry. In other words, it is the law of balancing the operating system. This is because if there is no requirement of balance in symmetry, the system tries to slide toward singularity and movement stops. However, the laws of the system do not allow singularity, and thus, they make movement eternal. We can call this the principle and necessity that contrasts the balance. The total size of the balancing contrasts represent the main structure of the system. In principle, when a main structure is divided, this division must be made equal for the symmetry to work. The structures that are not equally divided are balanced with main forces or passive structures. The moment of decision in the operation of our consciousness operates in the same way. This operation works as of the first moment on the matter and energy system of the universe. The existence of symmetry in the system of the universe is a principally structural phenomenon, and activeness-passiveness is its dynamic and moving form. In other words, it is the operating form of symmetry. We can also call it the activation of main forces, or the appearance of passive structures. The N (north) and S (south) poles of a magnet are structurally symmetrical and balanced with each other. Yet, the complex magnetic field that will emerge when you rapidly rotate the magnet at a certain speed is the active-passive operation in this rotation, and the holistic structure that emerges in the magnetic field movement with the magnet being the system itself. You cannot separate the structural and operational characteristics of this event while the magnet is rotating because what you will see is a rotating object with a variable magnetic field. In other words, you may be mistaken if you try to enter the system from outside. This means you will be very mistaken when you go from passive to active in reverse. However, you may have the chance to correctly understand this operation only if you make an analysis from inside to outside. In other words, you will more easily and effortlessly figure out the fact that it is a structure that emerges with the rotation of a two-polar magnet.

Other than such active-passive structures, there are also operations that depend on a transformation. The energy released when one helium atom is formed into two hydrogen atoms, or the heat and light that emerge from a burning object are examples of this. This law is one of the major operating laws in our consciousness. With this law, we can understand and explain what consciousness is, and how it operates in the most understandable way.

Let's try to best understand the concepts of active and passive and to explain why they can be important through some examples. As we all know, the Earth we live on has mass and gravity. It also revolves around its own axis at a speed of 1670 km, and magnetic fields emerge at its poles. We know that these are natural results, but we should not ignore the fact that there is a distinction and order. The magnetism here is the phenomenon that emerges depending on the objective structure and movement of the Earth. In other words, it is not the structure that brings itself into existence; it is the passive structure that depends on a formation. Here, the Earth is active and magnetism is passive.

If we ask, "Why is this important?", it's a similar scenario for our brain and thoughts – there is a cause-effect relationship of our consciousness. For example, if a person thinks that everything exists because he/she thinks, the law of active-passiveness is the evidence that everything he/she thinks cannot be true and exists, and our consciousness is passive, not active, in this existence. More clearly, something does not exist just because we think. Because something exists, we think about that existing structure and comprehend that it exists. In other words, we cannot create an existence that does not structurally exist by thinking. Thus, the fact that we think about things that do not exist does not mean what we think about does or will exist. Accordingly, the existence of magnetism is not the skill of magnetism itself; it is a passiveness depending on the rotation of the Earth. In fact, it would be an improper assumption and a mistake if magnetism thought by itself and said, "I would still exist if the Earth did not exist," and "The Earth exists thanks to me". Thus, knowing this will prevent our intellectual mistakes and wrong assumptions and will encourage us to think in a more realistic way, because our consciousness is also passive.

Here, we can briefly address the difference between the cause-effect operation and the active-passive operation. There is a transformation, differentiation, and conversion into a new formation in the cause-effect operation. For example, water vapour is condensed in the clouds, transforms into rain, and falls down on the Earth, or you heat water and water starts to evaporate. The system that operates in the occurrence stages of these events, for example, the system that operates in the process of heating water is the **active-passive** process, and this process indicates a (dynamic) moving process. With the completion of this process, the formation of cause-effect occurs.

When we burn paper, the paper burns moving along in the form of a line and the flame moves toward the unburnt area while the points it passes become ash. That linear area is the **activeness-passiveness**, in other words, the sudden transformation area. This area is the separation line between the paper that turned into ash and the paper that will continue to burn. This line is also the **symmetry line**, region, or area. In this case, it is both the active-passive and the symmetry area (the place where "burnt-unburnt" separation emerges).

Similarly, imagine that you got on a bus and assume that you sit facing the opposite direction of the bus's destination. The view that you will see is the view that the bus passes, not the view in the direction where the bus is going. Your viewpoint is like you are on the burning line of the paper (from the previous example used). While you are travelling with your back facing the direction you are going toward, what you see each moment is what you leave behind. What you leave behind is what has been lived and passed in time, and your back is turned to the future. You are moving between the **past and future**. In this case, you live the "**moment**" between the past and future and this is valid for each "**moment**" every day you live.

We live the "**moment**" right on the line between the past and future and that exact "**moment**" is the plane of symmetry and the cross-section "**moment**". That exact "**moment**" is also our **consciousness** "**moment**" that we feel, perceive, think, and are aware of. Our consciousness structure here is **passive** as the continuity of the past and **active** for the future. In other words, our consciousness in the future will take over our consciousness at that "**moment**". However, at this moment, we don't know what our consciousness will be in the future.

If the **activeness-passiveness** and the plane or **area of symmetry** did not exist, our consciousness could not occur. This is because in this case, comparison and meaning awareness would not emerge. If the contrast of different symmetry concepts, just like the part of the paper on the burning line (burnt-unburnt) did not exist, the difference, consciousness, and idea that the paper is burnt and unburnt could not emerge because our consciousness could not perceive them as different.

Another example would be the **interface** of the software and the image when a video's digital software is reflected on the computer screen. A part of both transformations exist in both the software and the image. Our consciousness is a structure which combines both the neuron software in our brain, as well as the space-time software that we perceive with our five senses (receptor senses), and the consciousness of existing in the cosmos in the "moment".

Our neuron software starts with genetic codes and includes our subconsciousness and defence mechanisms, as well as our autonomous system software. This is also a system that covers our connections with our outer world, expectations, and responsibilities, and operates based on memory. In other words, the image we see at the moment we blink is like seeing a view in a video frame. What defines this view is our neuron software. The software regarding the awareness of all this and the formation of meaning are events that occur simultaneously with our consciousness. Our consciousness' space-time software includes our position and conditions at that "moment" and what we feel at that moment, these are the data points. The other most important data is our cosmos consciousness that we are connected to like a navigation (the causality consciousness of liveliness, existence). The structure that makes us human and separates us from the other living creatures is that we have the cosmos (Creator) consciousness, in other words, the causality consciousness.

Consciousness and "moment" are in symmetry with each other and cannot be thought of separately. Without one, the other cannot exist (the law of necessity), and the consciousness cannot create meaning and provide integrity. The thing that will be active for our consciousness to emerge in the future is all of the space-time conditions of today, our biochemistry, and our current consciousness.

If someone claims that they saw something about the future, this is unrealistic, just like the fact that you claim you can see the road although you sit in the bus with your back turned to the travelling direction. It is pretty clear that this is intentional and that this claim is absurd because scientifically, it is absolutely impossible to see or know the future due to the infinite variables and combinations of the events that may be related to the future.

We will have sorted out the wrong formations in our consciousness by looking at events and phenomena on a scientific basis. As a way of categorising what can or cannot be possible in life. We will explain and portray that our consciousness is a passive structure in almost every subject. Perhaps, an example would help to understand.

Our consciousness is a formation that is attached to our body (brain), and consequently, it is a passive structure that is formed later and is attached to the brain. For example, after drinking alcohol, our consciousness cannot prevent our brain from being affected by alcohol. This is because our brain is active and our consciousness is passive. When our active structure is affected, our passive structure will inevitably be affected by the situation. However, doing this in reverse is unrealistic. In other words, you cannot numb your consciousness by only thinking, without consuming alcohol. The passive structure is the active structure itself, and this structure cannot be operated in reverse.

Therefore, the claims that people can be treated through meditation for every matter are not correct. The positive effects of meditation on the regulation of the energy system operating in the body are limited. Thus, the claim that every negative factor can be regulated through meditation or thought is limited.

The most important thing that we should understand is that not everything our consciousness deems possible is possible, and we should never ignore this fact.

Time

Movement, change, transformation speed, and time

(The formation of the "Cosmos Time" will be explained in the quantum section.)

The concept of time has been perceived throughout the history of mankind, and humans have tried to define what it is. It has been associated with the universe and nature depending on the advancements made in science and technology and has tried to be understood through these associations and the connections between them.

Because all concepts are intertwined and connected to each other, many things have been confused and what we should understand with the concept of "time" could never accurately be explained or defined. In order to correctly explain and understand time, first we need to understand some key operations in the universe, and then define time in accordance with these explanations.

Today, space and time are concepts that are considered combined and are regarded as an intertwining texture. As space and time are regarded as the same texture, evaluation is made with the assumption that the circumstances that affect space will also affect time. However, the relationship between space and time is different from what is known today, so to fully understand this difference, it is necessary to have a good understanding of the operation of the universe and make a definition within the scope of this understanding. Gaining a good understanding of the operation of the universe requires correct analysis of the laws and principles of the universe.

Each phenomenon or formation in the universe has a structural dimension and a dimension that we call the characteristics of this structural dimension, and there are other phenomena and structures that are formed within their operation (movement). If we call their structural 'make-up' or 'parts' **active** structures, and the characteristics of these structures are the structures' **passive** forms. Passive structures exist depending on the existence and movement of the main structure, and ultimately shape their characteristics.

This is an attachment based on the necessity that one should exist when the other exists, not in the way that one creates another.

For instance, water (H_2O) in a pot has structural characteristics. When you heat the pot, the water molecules take energy and gain different characteristics. The structure of water (H_2O) does not change but its energy structure, in other words, its passive structure, changes. For example, if you pour boiling water on a flower, you kill the flower. We can then deduce that a definition like "**water is life and the source of life**" is not correct under all circumstances.

As you can understand from the example above, we realise that we are easily mistaken and don't fully understand some realities when we examine events and phenomena from a holistic perspective. While we are heating water in the pot, other operations also occur that we don't always take into account, in fact, on occasion we ignore them. While we are heating the water in the pot, gas is burned on the stove under the pot and heats the pot. The source of the heat on the stove is structurally inflammable and is an active source that generates heat. The heat that is formed when the gas is burned emerges as passive and heats the pot. While the gas is burning, heat and light emerge as passive and heat the pot as the structural gas molecules react with the oxygen in the air and transform into other molecules. Although the thermal energy that emerges as the gas is burned is a passive structure, it is active in terms of heating the pot as the phenomenon that heats the pot. In other words, although heat itself passively exists in the burning of the gas, it is active in heating the water in the pot as the phenomenon that heats the water. In this case, heat is both active and passive.

The heating of the water in the pot is also an activity-passivity process because there is a temperature difference between the temperature one second before and the temperature one second after. In other words, there is an increase in the temperature and we interpret the occurrence of this increase with **time** passing.

If you pay attention, all these events indicate a series of operations and the existence of a movement.

For instance, gas is burned, chemical reactions occur, heat emerges, and the temperature of the water in the pot gradually increases. Whatever the operation and movement is, we think that the most important factor is **time**; what makes us understand this entire movement is time itself, and **time** exists as a structural phenomenon. Some might think that this scenario could not take place in the absence of time and progress of time, that everything occurs within time and we proceed in time. We evaluate and define time as a real phenomenon that exists on its own. **However, we are mistaken**. We will understand the reason for this mistake, when we correctly define phenomena and operations.

For instance, we are mistaken if we look at the concept of m (matter, mass) in the formula $E=m.C^2$, which we all know, in a holistic approach. This formula comes to the generalisation that "Every element with the same mass also has the same level of energy". However, even if the mass of 1 kg carbon element and 1 kg uranium element are equal, the energy that they will release cannot be equal. This is because these elements' structural characteristics and formation energy levels are different. For example, the formation energy of the uranium element is higher than the formation energy of the carbon element. In other words, the fact that both elements have equal mass does not mean their energy levels will be equal. This is because we immediately understand that they cannot be equal. If we look at the endothermic or exothermic reaction characteristics of a thermonuclear fusion event. We can understand this from the law of the conservation of energy. Hence, we will also understand that if we talk about energy, we have to take into account the internal formation energy level of the material that creates that mass. Accordingly, we should take the internal energy structure of the structure that creates the mass into account; in other words, we should multiply it by its own internal energy coefficient (k) ($E=m(k).C^2$), for the formula to be correct.

A holistic point of view similar to the point of view on the formula portrayed above can also mislead scientists or make it difficult to understand some facts. The concept of time also has a similar nature and has not always been understood throughout history. If we address and evaluate the concept of time as we know it today, we can notice that there are no answers for many questions and understand that we have made mistakes at some point. If time is a one-way arrow that exists on its own and moves forward, no speed in the universe should pass the arrow of time. This is because no speed can be thought of and identified higher than the flow rate of time. If there is a higher speed than the flow rate of time, then the meaning of time disappears.

Quantum entanglement law looks at time speed and the communication speed between particles. This communication is a phenomenon that occurs too fast to be explained by our concept of time. This is because the communication between the entangled particles at the distance of millions of light years occurs at almost infinitely high speeds according to our concept of time. In other words, communication at those long distances occurs at this speed. If the flow rate of time is that high, that means we do not know what time really is, and we do not know the communication laws and communication networks of the universe that provide this fast communication. In other words, it means we know this entanglement law but we do not know how it works. However, what happens here is confusing the structural phenomenon and operation laws and is incorrect. Our mistake regarding the concept of time stems from the fact that we cannot separate structural phenomena and functional phenomena; in other words, we do not know the characteristics of the **active-passive** operation. Because our consciousness system works in the active-passive operation, we make similar mistakes in every area of life. We should correctly understand activeness-passiveness to correctly understand this operation.

For example, if the movement of the universe stopped for 10 seconds, would time continue to exist?

If time stopped for 10 seconds, would the movement of the universe stop, too?

If time stopped for 10 seconds, could we still continue to think?

If our consciousness stopped for 10 seconds, would we still be aware of the fact that time passes?

As can be seen, these cannot be considered separately, and one of them cannot be meaningful and defined without the other. In the end, one is a structural movement and the other is the meaning dimension that interprets and understands this movement.

Time: Is a dimension of meaning and concept that we perceive the operation of the movement in terms of process when a movement occurs. **Time is a concept that depends on the occurrence of movement; it is not a phenomenon that exists on its own.** In other words, it is a meaning dimension that cannot exist without a movement, and generates depending on the occurrence of a movement. Just like the fact that our consciousness cannot emerge and we cannot understand and know whether there is a concept of life without the movement of our brain.

We know that there is a time whether or not we exist, because we know that the universe has its own movement outside of us and we evaluate this movement process as time. The fact that the universe has a phenomenon of time in its own movement means the universe has its own phenomenon of time outside of us. This situation will be further explained in the quantum section.

For us, time is a perception of movement that emerges depending on our brain's speed of movement. In other words, the duration of being aware and comprehending what we think is the concept of a moment of time for us.

Our concept of time is a concept that exists within the concept of the universe.

When we think, we cannot think by not using our brain, as if this process wasn't a product of our brain. This is like the mistake that we would still exist even if our parents did not exist.

This mistake is also valid for our concept of time – we think time always exists on its own, independently of movement, and we are mistaken. What brings time into existence is movement. If there is no movement, there will be no change, and the perception that time exists will not emerge anyway.

The movement speed of each formation in the universe is different, and the concept of time of that movement is different depending on this movement speed. The concept of time in the expansion speed of the universe and the concept of time in the growth rate of a tree are different. This is because their movement speed is different from each other. Even if this speed is a million times faster than light, it has its own concept of time. Even if movement is at an infinite speed, the concept of time will also be infinite depending on this speed. Consequently, time is not a phenomenon that operates independently of movement and exists on its own, it is a phenomenon that emerges and appears depending on movement itself. In short, time cannot exist without movement.

If the Big Bang did not occur, time would not exist either. So, what is the answer to the question "If everything stopped after the Big Bang and movement did not exist, would time still exist"? Time would not exist.

To understand this well, think of the universe as a "**stopped**" clock on the wall. If that clock remained stopped on that wall forever, time would not have emerged and would have stopped forever. As long as that clock stayed on that wall without working, it would not have been possible for time to emerge.

As of the moment when the clock works, with the start of a movement, a movement speed will exist and that movement speed will be perceived as time. Accordingly, the perception of transition from the position a moment before to the position a moment after is our perception of time. The perception that there is a progression, is the perception that we define as time.

Because the concept of time is a phenomenon that depends on movement, it is not an objective phenomenon that will be affected by the texture of space, spatial difference, or gravitational force. As every clock that you make to measure time will be an objective structure, it will be natural that they are affected by gravitation, speed, or other characteristics of the universe. This is because every clock that is made will have a matter and energy structure and it is natural that this objective structure is affected by the universal conditions.

Nevertheless, the fact that the material that you use while making the clock is affected by the universal conditions does not mean that the concept of time is also affected. We can explain this situation with the similarity between mathematical concepts and the concept of time. If you write the number "3" on a piece of paper and throw the paper in a black hole event horizon, the paper will stretch, being affected by the gravitation of the black hole, and even if the number "3" stretches depending on the stretching of the paper, this does not mean the real number "3" in mathematics will also stretch. Similarly, the consciousness of mathematics is a structure that exists depending on movement. Without movement, the structure that will understand movement cannot emerge, and as a result the consciousness structure that creates mathematics information does not emerge either. Mathematics itself is a phenomenon that already exists principally in the operation of the universe. However, if we do not have consciousness; if we do not have a movement, we cannot be aware of this existence.

As time is a concept that emerges as a result of movement, the concept of "time" in the space-time theory and the theory that time is affected by gravitation are incorrect.

This is because the concept of time is not a structural and objective phenomenon that exists on its own as fixed on the texture of the universe, everywhere in the universe.

To understand this better, let's use the example of being affected by the magnetic field. Both aluminium and iron elements are metal but they have different magnetic characteristics. Thus, we cannot conclude that aluminium will be drawn to a magnet because it is metal, just based on the fact that a magnet attracts the element of iron. Similarly, as space and time are different concepts, it will not be correct to assume that time will also be affected by gravitation as because of the fact that space is affected by gravitation.

This is because time is not a structural phenomenon, it is a phenomenon that emerges as a result of the movement of a structural phenomenon.

What is affected by gravitation is not time; it is the movement of the structural phenomenon. For instance, when you drink alcohol, what is affected by alcohol is not our consciousness but our brain that creates our consciousness. As our brain is affected by alcohol, our consciousness is also affected. It is a mistake to ignore our brain and assume that our consciousness exists on its own and is directly affected by alcohol.

A cannonball moves, losing its initial speed when it comes out of the barrel, and its speed gradually decreases. The fact that the cannonball slows down should be explained not only by the fact that time slows down, but also the fact that the phenomena of time depending on this speed slows down. As we analyse events with our own fixed perception of time, we define all movement speeds according to the movement speed of our own brain. So, according to the time that we accept, all other concepts of time should of course be relative. This is because the movement speed of each formation in the universe is different from the movement speed of our brain. It is a mistake to evaluate time as a phenomenon that exists on its own, covers everything, and has its own constant speed.

This main mistake about time is that movement (speed) is defined according to time.

In other words, defining the active structure according to the passive structure.

However, the passive structure does not exist on its own and should be defined according to the active structure.

In other words, movement and speed should be defined not according to time; time itself should be defined according to movement (speed).

This is because when you define the magnetism created by the rotation of the Earth, you should not define the Earth according to magnetism; you should define the magnetism according to the Earth. Just like the fact that our consciousness cannot exist on its own without our brain. It would be incorrect to claim that our consciousness would exist without our brain.

Claiming that time would exist without movement is the same thing.

In summary, time is not a phenomenon that exists on its own; it is a phenomenon that emerges depending on movement.

As it is a concept that emerges depending on movement, not an objective phenomenon, it is not a structure that will be affected by the physical conditions of the universe. Just like mathematical operations such as multiplication and division will not lose their functions being affected by a black hole; the concept of time is not a phenomenon that will be affected by gravitation. In short, 2×2 is 4 on Earth, on Jupiter, or in a black hole.

This is because gravitation cannot twist, bend and change the conceptual function of the operations such as multiplication and division.

As the first movement is the Big Bang, the beginning of time is the Big Bang. In other words, the beginning of time is the Big Bang because we do not know the period before it. We call this first "moment" of transformation the critical "moment" and that first critical moment is both the "moment" when the transformation from one structure to another structure and the "moment" when all universal laws that we know and do not know started to emerge. The laws and principles through which matter and energy transformation starts, and how and to what it will transform into is determined; in short, this "moment" includes everything in the universe. This "moment" is also the first "moment" of the concept that we know as the concept of "time". The concept of "moment" is a meaning dimension that moves as the matter and energy transformation process continues.

It would be more accurate to consider the concept of "moment" as a movie camera that shoots and records what happens on the stage, independently of what happens on the stage when a movie is made on a stage. We understand the existence of time from the transformation speed and movement of things and the change in the conditions.

We understand that time passes when we observe a snowflake falling, the definition that time is affected by movement and gravitation in Albert Einstein's Theory of Relativity is a mistaken definition which today's science takes as reference. According to this theory, what is measured as time is an objective concept. Because this is an objective definition, it is based on the assumption that the gravitation of a black hole can bend space, and time. Accordingly, the material with which we measure time is an objective material and because it has energy and mass, we interpret the fact that it is affected by gravitation as the fact that time is also affected by gravitation.

Even if we throw a digital clock in a black hole event horizon and the operation of the digital clock really slows down and comes to a point of stopping due to the gravitation of the black hole, what will slow down and stop in there is not time; it is the value measured depending on the objectivity of that clock.

It is necessary to use an objective timer (clock) and a concept of time to make a measurement because measuring time is an indispensable concept that we need for our life. Yet, this objective concept of time based on what we accept is flawed for science-based solutions.

According to Albert Einstein's Theory of Relativity, it is predicted that in a rocket moving close to the speed of light, we would age at different times than our twin. This means, in a way, my twin's heart would beat twenty times while my heart beats 100 times.

Yes, even if our twin went billions of kilometres away from us, their heart would beat at the same rate as ours; or even if it beat at a different rate, this would not be an event depending on the fact that time slows down, but an event depending on speed. However, whatever the speed is, both of us will get old in the same way within the cosmos time scale. This is because if we spend one year within the cosmos time scale, our twin will also spend one year. Thus, we have to take into account the fact of time of the cosmos outside of our own perception of time.

The concept of real "moment" of the conceptual time and cosmos time can be explained as follows: For example, if we take a photo 10 seconds after the current moment based on the classic time. Let's try to understand what will happen at that "moment" of taking the photo:

The "moment" when the shutter of the camera takes the photo is actually also a cross-section "moment" of space-time. Let's identify and define this cross-section.

Space is that "moment" that spatially involves and draws "everything". It is the "moment" of presence in the rotation of the Earth in its orbit. This is also the "moment" when the sun is in its orbit. It is the "moment" when the galaxy, stars, and planets around a black hole exist. It is the "moment" of rotation of another galaxy billions of light years away. It is the "moment" when the light coming from the sun falls on the photo frame that the photo is taken.

It is the way that everything else that exists in the universe is at the "moment" when we take the photo. In other words, space is a cross-section "moment" of time when we take that photo (the space-time layer). This moment is also the conscious "moment" of our consciousness and the "moment" of symmetry of space-time. It is the "moment" when our consciousness comprehends this symmetry. In short, it is the form of the current shape of space-time (its software form) defined by our brain and turned into a photo.

What you see like a vizor when you blink is the cross-section of space-time. This "moment" is the "moment" when you comprehend and define what you see in your consciousness.

When you correctly understand the concept of "moment", you will understand that you cannot go to the past or the future physically and the idea of time travel is irrational. When this concept is correctly understood, the real meaning and importance of the second entropy law of thermodynamics will also be understood.

Understanding the real core of the concept of "moment" is extremely important to understanding the law and operation of **active and passive. Understanding the activeness and passiveness well nullifies the fact that people put forward thousands of unrealistic and abnormal ideas about existence and creation and prevents the waste of time and resources regarding scientific research that will not yield any results.** Moreover, it will be understood and comprehended that numerous made-up creation stories that have come from the past until today cannot be real. The negative results of these stories on humans' lives will also be eliminated.

The concept of time means these "moments" progress by being attached to each other; it is one-way and cannot be operated in reverse. In fact, what we call life is living the "moment". This is because our experiences are the "moments" of the past, and the "moments" that will come are the "moments" that we have not yet lived. We live right in the middle of this, between the past and the present.

Therefore, the concept of "moment" is both active and passive, like our consciousness. The activeness and passiveness of the "consciousness and moment" are inseparable and are the symmetry of each other. All formations in the universe are **passive** according to the past, and **active** according to the future.

The Law Of Symmetry

The system of the universe regarding the dimension of matter and energy works like the pans of a scale. The energy systems in the universe try to balance the energy structure in their own symmetry and acquire a neutral structure. For instance, if you mix a glass of hot water with a glass of cold water, heat transfer begins and continues until they reach an equal temperature. When the temperature becomes equal, the transfer of heat stops. The temperature point where the temperatures of both glasses (hot and cold) is the point of symmetry.

In another example, if a stone rolls from the peak of a mountain, the stone's potential energy is balanced with its kinetic energy, and only then does the stone stop. This operation in nature or the universe also occurs in the dimension of consciousness in humans' in their daily lives. People experience the movement of this system, which operates in the universe, and creates thought combinations to balance it.

The law of symmetry is one of the basic laws of our consciousness system. We act according to the operation of these laws when we form a behavioural model, make a decision, or make a choice. The determinant of what we live and feel about justice, fairness, or injustice is the energy operation of the law of symmetry. The fact that we suffer, feel sad, or happy or at peace depends on the system inside us which operates like the pans of a scale. This operation is about which pan outweighs another, and what we do and say to balance it. In other words, an operation which stems from the electric potential difference in our neurons. The fact that we want to hurt someone when they hurt us, we lose our trust in someone when they lie to us, or we want to respect someone who respects us, are all results and examples of this operation.

We can talk about two types of software that affect this operation. One of them is our basic instinct software that works in our basic software codes. The other is our principles and behavioural model software that we choose as a reference. What we do or say is formed by a blending operation of these two types of software and enduring the balance that is the most appropriate for the situation. Our biological and psychological basic defence mechanisms are a part of this operation. This operation is a system that depends on the energy difference and is aimed to balance it.

Nutrition, reproduction, and sheltering (protection), which are considered basic instincts, are common impulses in humans and animals and the operation of these impulses occurs in the same software. This operation involves the working systems that depend on certain principles and parameters. This operation also has a consciousness. For instance, prey-hunter, attack-defence, danger-trust. . .

In humans, except for this commonly operating consciousness system, there is the consciousness of interpretation, description, and preference. The consciousness of comparing and reasoning is in question and this consciousness stems from the law of symmetry. What makes people human is consciousness. Although it seems to work in a very complex way, the system that operates in all humans is a common one. This system also works according to certain principles and laws and one of the most important of these is the law of symmetry. While the receptor stimuli of the five senses are analysed in our brain, operation of the law of symmetry occurs in several different ways. The receptor energy operation of this analysis occurs as scale-balance, pendulum-swinging, and sine wave. We will see how this law operates and affects how we behave together when we address the subjects in daily lives and people's beliefs. We will discuss the subjects of justice, fairness, sincerity, responsibility, and belief, which are among the basic subjects in social life. We will comprehend how they operate on the scientific basis and really get to understand and appreciate our own identity better.

2

PRINCIPLES OF CONSCIOUSNESS AND QUANTUM

(Meaning and Cosmos-Formation of Time-Principles of Stability and Quantum)

As a principle, we know that everything in the universe is, and will be, moving.

We also know that meaning or consciousness are principles that emerge as a result of movement.

Consciousness potentially exists, but movement is necessary for it to become identifiable and understandable.

As this movement is infinite, let's try to understand its infrastructure.

A movement must be circular (orbital motion) to be infinite. This is because every non-circular (periodical) movement has a beginning and an end. However, circular movement is in an infinite cycle because it does not have a beginning or an end.

Two possibilities are required for an object moving in a circular orbit to be observed as stable.

The first option is stability when there really is no movement.

However, where there is no movement; time, meaning and consciousness do not exist, this is impossible (the laws of the universe do not allow this).

The second option is that this object moves in that orbit so fast that it completes its cycle when it spins around the orbit; it comes to the point from which it starts to move, no time passes in this movement, and we do not notice this movement as it is very quick.

In other words, the object moves so fast that we observe it as stable at the same point, as if it does not move at all.

In theory, for this to occur, it is necessary that the object is as big as infinity and the orbit is as small as infinity (the paradox of symmetry of our consciousness).

If such a situation really existed, time and meaning dimensions would not emerge even though there is movement.

In this theoretical phenomenon, the speed required for time and meaning to emerge must be a limited speed instead of being infinite. In other words, this speed should be constant in a way to ensure that a gap difference emerges while the object completes its tour and comes to the same point.

This speed is the constant movement speed of the universe and this gap is the emergence of the concept of a "moment" of time in the universe.

The practical equivalent of this theoretical circular movement on the basis of quantum is the quantum vibration (swinging, wave motion).

This operation in the quantum energy or information dimension constitutes and reveals the definition and meaning of dimension. In other words, this operation is the infrastructure that shows there is movement and it creates the meaning and consciousness dimension. **This also indicates the emergence of the concept of "time".**

In other words, quantum vibration is the real time concept of the universe and has a speed beyond our perception.

If the universe exists today, no structure existing in the universe is durable. In other words, the fact that something is durable means the universe freezes and movement ends. Such an option cannot be possible (the laws and principles of the universe do not allow this).

Yet, because our perception system cannot comprehend this movement, we believe that some things can be stable, and we are mistaken. For example, we see a tree at the same point for years and think that it is stable.

However, that tree moves along with the Earth as the Earth rotates around its axis and around the Sun at a speed of thousands of km/h – it photosynthesises, and changes occur in its cells. However, because it does not move like us, we think that it is stable compared to us, and we are mistaken. **Thus, we cannot evaluate the reality of the events and phenomena through our perceptions.** Even if it is not reflected in our perception, we should comprehend that there is an operation over those phenomena.

In the quantum information structural dimension, an option such as, "exists and does not exist" is out of the question for a structural phenomenon. The option that "**it either exists or does not exist**" is valid for structural phenomena and we should not confuse structural phenomena and operational phenomena.

For instance, in a coin flip, the possibility that the coin comes up heads or tails and the possibility that the coin exists or does not exist are not the same. Clearly, a coin can indeed flip up both heads or tails but it cannot exist and not exist. One is a structural phenomenon and the other is an operational phenomenon of that structure (the active-passive operation). If there are no coins (factor) in place, the possibility of flipping a heads or tails does not exist anyway, because the possibility of heads or tails depends on the condition that a coin exists. Hence, as a structural option, something "**either exists or does not exist**".

Similarly, there is no possibility for an electron to be at two places at the same time.

There is a possibility that an electron is seen at two different places due to movement uncertainty.

But the electron itself cannot be at two places at the same time, because it is contrary to the laws of thermodynamics and the principles of movement.

This is the confusion of structural phenomena with operational phenomena or an observation error.

The fact that an electron exists in two places at the same time means either the division of the electron into two or the creation of a new electron. Which is not possible.

If a creature exists, only then can we talk about its characteristics and operation.

It is impossible to talk about the characteristics and operation of a creature that does not exist, but generally we ignore this and can make incorrect assumptions. **The main reason for this is that we evaluate non-structural passive structures as if they are structural phenomena and escape from awareness – and we are mistaken.**

In fact, our imagination or the fact that we believe in the existence of things that do not exist is due to this operation. This is because our consciousness is also a part of this active-passive operation.

This is the situation of 2+2=2, 2×2=2, or 2–2=2.

For instance, if you only have 2 electrons and add another 2 electrons that do not already exist, the result will again be 2 electrons. This is because if you add the non-existing 2 electrons to the system as if they exist, you will try to create the 2 electrons that do not exist in the system and think there will be 4 electrons. The result should be 4 in terms of the principles of mathematics but it will be 2 in the structural reality. This is because you already have 2 electrons, and you bring the other 2 electrons into existence presumptively and add up.

Similarly, you cannot have 1 god + 1 god = 2 gods, or 1 universe + 1 universe = 2 universes. Or you cannot obtain 2 black holes by adding 1 black hole to another black hole.

Again, principally, you cannot add, subtract, or multiply a structure with itself. In other words, you cannot make an apple disappear by subtracting it from itself. For instance, you cannot have 1 apple – 1 apple = 0 apples because the laws of thermodynamics do not allow for this.

You can only divide a structural phenomenon. This division option, and the process of creating pieces in a whole, occurs thanks to the existence of the law of symmetry. No matter how many pieces you divide, each piece is divided with its own symmetry or is divided symmetrically to the main structure. For instance, no matter how much you divide a magnet, it will be divided with its magnetic symmetry until the last piece you can divide.

The determinant of what exists and does not exist in the system is the laws of the system, like in the laws of symmetry, or in the laws of thermodynamics. When we presumptively accept the existence of the things that do not exist and add them to the system, these references will make us understand that this assumption is wrong. These are the laws and principles of the universe.

The operation that we call the quantum operation and the operation of the universe are actually the same. This is because the operation of consciousness is actually a quantum operation. Thus, if we can understand our consciousness, we will also understand quantum. In this context, one of them is active and the other is its passive form and they are intertwined. One is existing, the other is creating, and they bring each other into existence. One is the dimension of energy, universal laws, principles and information, and the other is the dimension of meaning, comprehension, and consciousness.

The things that emerge in the movement process of time, information (the information of how mathematics and basic forces of the universe will operate) and the energy at that moment are the meaning, or consciousness, of that movement. In other words, it is the event of the emergence and comprehension of the meaning that a movement exists.

Here, the basic forces, universal laws, information, and speed of movement (time) are the invariant parameters of the system. These are the constant parameters that create the content integrity of our consciousness.

We can think of our hardware like a piano. A piano has a lot of keys and we hear the sound of the note "do" when the note "do" is pressed. Our emotion and consciousness systems are also like this. When we press on the note "do", the piano will not make a sound other than that of the note "do". Just as the fact that the piano must make the sound of "do" when the note "do" is pressed, the operation of our consciousness is also administered with such principles of necessity. If the principles of necessity did not exist and the piano made the sound of "mi" when we pressed on the note "do", we could not form a content integrity due to this inconsistency and the meaning of the notes would disappear.

As can be seen, without the constants and references of the universe, our consciousness would not have meaning.

The most important conclusion should be as follows: It is impossible for us humans, who think through certain

references, to understand the consciousness of the consciousness that creates these references.

In other words, to understand why the note making the sound "do" makes the sound "do", it is necessary to know the universal information of all constants of the universe.

As comprehension of this requires going out of the universe and looking at it from outside, this is impossible. Thus, humans' search for causality for the laws of necessity is a mistake.

Every argument that they will take as an answer will be incorrect or insufficient. **This is because necessity is active, while causality is passive and cannot be operated in reverse.**

In other words, what creates causality is already a necessity, and it is impossible for us to comprehend the consciousness of necessity.

You can attribute a causality to a necessity and explain it. However, you cannot go in reverse and explain a necessity with a causality. This is because attributing a necessity to a causality means **acceptance**. However, every acceptance includes limited information and does not reflect reality. The analyses based on acceptances that do not include a confirmation based on the universal laws cannot be real; they must include inconsistencies and errors.

This is the technical infrastructure of beliefs and the philosopher Plato's description of shadows on the wall. Acceptances that are not based on reality are the reverse operation of the active–passive operation.

(The relationship of acceptances with consciousness and belief will be discussed in detail in the Causality section.)

The meaning of acceptance is that you believe in something in your way as if you see the objects that create the shadows on the wall, even if you sit with your back to those objects when you look at the shadows on the wall.

As we do not know what the shadow reflected on the wall belongs to, how will we understand what type of a reality this shadow belongs to? Based on this obscurity, humanity has believed in non-existing, unrealistic, and unreasonable things and has been out of touch with reality throughout history (for example, mythological gods).

However, no matter what creates those shadows, they will be the realities that the universal laws allow.

In other words, even if we do not know what the object that creates the shadow is, knowing that it should be a real object is much more important for us. This is because no phenomenon or formation which is impossible according to the universal laws can be real. Thus, comprehending that everything that has a shadow on a wall should be real is much more important.

The universal laws are the laws and operations that determine what the structure to which we sit with our back to will be. For example, in the period when Plato lived, many things were unknown, and people may have imagined that shadow on the wall as a bird with 20 wings, or a creature with 20 arms and legs. Similarly, today, people believe in the existence of impossible things and imaginary realities based on the justification of "**Why would it not exist if I think about it?**" and seriously deceive themselves. They even go further and impose their imaginations on humanity as if they are real. However, what they ignore and miss are the universal laws and principles of feasibility. While the universal laws are obvious, it is impossible for the formations that these laws do not allow to exist.

Let's analyse and clarify this subject with an example that will enable a better understanding of this type of reality, and the reality of quantum. An example similar to Plato's shadows on the wall ,and try to understand the operation.

Imagine for a moment that you faint and then wake up in a pitch black room. Assume that sounds are coming from the room, there is a motion, and some things that you cannot understand happen. Your predictions regarding what is happening or what will happen are left to your imagination. You can think of billions of things that may or may not happen in this room. So, in this uncertainty about what is happening in the room, how will you learn whether or not what you think really exists, or whether or not what you think is a figment of your imagination? Or will you believe in the existence of the things that you want to believe exist in the room?

Imagine that just as you think about this, the lights are turned on and the room is illuminated. Now, what you see will be the reality of that room. Everything that does not exist in that room and that you think exists in your imagination will lose its meaning, and you will see what is in the room. Everything that exists in that room will be the things that are possible according to the universal law. In other words, what distinguishes your imagination from reality are the universal laws.

The possibility of everything being real in your imagination depends only on whether they comply with the universal laws. Any formations that do not comply with the universal laws cannot exist and occur in that room. Thus, the silhouette of every shadow on Plato's wall of shadows must be real. In other words, the necessity and fact that the things that will exist there even if you sit with your back to them are the structures complying with the universal laws.

In summary, the fact that a person convinces themself about, and defends, as they want the existence of a formation which the universal laws will not allow to exist cannot be realistic and correct. This is because what makes the existence of a formation meaningful is already the universal laws. Mentioning reality and ignoring the universal laws is an absurd situation.

> **"The situation that we cannot know what is in that room before the lights are turned on is the case of quantum uncertainty. In other words, the case that everything the universal laws potentially allow can exist. What we see when the lights are turned on is quantum reality. In other words, the situation where possibilities are clarified, and turned into reality, and become truly observable."**

Now, let's evaluate the event that has happened here over principles and list our conclusions.

If there was no light and the room was not illuminated, the phenomena that exist in that room would have no familiarity or meaning for us. This is because we could not know the size, colour, and shape of any of the objects in the room without light. As we did not know the objects in the room, we could not question and try to understand why they were different and what the infrastructure features of the operation that created those differences were.

If we were not in the room, we would have no idea what was in the room.

In other words, if we were not in the room, the phenomena in the room would be a situation that we were unaware of because it would be outside of us whether they were illuminated or not.

This means a structure that understands and comprehends the events happening and interprets them should first exist for definition and meaning to be able to exist. In other words, if we do not exist, we cannot talk about the existence or absence of a phenomenon or a consciousness anyway.

Nevertheless, we know that there is another reality and consciousness outside of us whether we exist or not. This is because if such a reality and consciousness did not exist, the consciousness and phenomena that bring us into existence would not exist, and consequently we would not exist because they did not exist. In other words, our existence requires the existence of an entity before us.

This means we should analyse events from these two points of view. **One of them is the operation regarding our existence. The other is the operation outside of us, whether we exist or not.** In the end, the system that brings us into existence is a system that operates externally, not from us. As a result, we should try to evaluate our own existence over the existence of this system. We should understand the principles and laws of the system that operates us and the system that operates outside of us to fully understand why the system that brings us into existence does so.

When we understand the mutual operation of these two systems, we establish the cause-effect relationship of the event. All laws that exist in the universe also operate for us. When we understand our own operation, we also understand the operation outside of us. Therefore, the universal laws are indispensable and every thought and approach contrary to the universal laws moves us away from reality.

Whatever we believe about why we exist, disregarding the universal laws, it will not be real and correct, because there will not be any accurate information source for us to question and confirm. The answer to the question "Where will we learn the meaning and information of why we exist?" is again our own operation. Our existence is based on the operation of the principle that "**An object cannot create and define its own objectivity**". In other words, it is based on the reason infrastructure of the beliefs' discourse that "God is the one that created everything".

If there is a God and no other creature exists other than God, then who would know the existence of God (The case of singularity)?

This fact that God is known is the movement of the existence in the universe (necessity of symmetry).

In this movement, consciousness (meaning) emerges, defines the creature, and makes it known. We, as all living or non-living creatures, are the creatures that interpret and know the power that creates the universe or brings it into existence in both the passive form and the symmetry of it.

The meaning of the operation of the cosmos is the emergence of a passive structure in the movement of the main structure (cosmos), its emergence as the symmetry of that moving structure, and the fact that it brings meaning and recognition to that structure.

The situation in question is similar to the fact that our consciousness emerges in the movement of our brain and makes our existence known. In this case, the conclusion that "**The sum of everything is God itself**" is not that incorrect.

No matter for what purpose we exist or have been created, we should learn and conclude what it is, from the operation of the system that works within us.

For example, practices such as lying, betrayal, deception, torture, humiliation and arrogance disturb the entirety of humanity. On the other hand, practices such as love, respect, peace, tolerance, fellowship, justice, fairness and equity make us happy.

If we can separate them and choose which one can be appropriate for us, this will be the causality consciousness of our existence. We all know that the system within us promotes us to be good people, no matter what purpose we exist for. If we know this, then we can easily conclude that the system inside us operates in the direction of us being good people without need for any other reason.

When we understand that, we also comprehend that to act according to the consciousness that operates the system in question and to understand it.

Let's get back to the dark room and quantum reality to better understand this situation. Let's pretend that your memory is suddenly reset and you return to a position when you first came into the world while you are sitting in that dark room. Will the things you see in the room have meaning for you? For example, how will you interpret a table, chair, or television? Or will it be meaningless to you?

From this we can understand that what we refer to as information is the accumulations that we learn in the operation of the universal laws, which creates a cause-effect relationship by compiling and bringing them together, and records them. Whether or not we understand, whether or not we record, the movement of the universal laws operate based on certain principles and they all constitute the system's own information.

We cannot know in advance the movement that will occur a thousand years later. However, the information of a movement after a thousand years potentially exists in the system itself and it will be the information that will be revealed a thousand years later. Even if we roughly predict what can happen in line with these principles, only the process itself will determine what that information will be.

What we actually try to do is to understand the behaviours of the phenomenon and operation laws, make conclusions and definitions based on them. No matter what happens a thousand years later, it will be the information that will emerge as a result of the movement of the universal laws. Everything that will happen will occur in accordance with these laws and principles and nothing will be coincidental, even if they have an infinite number of variables and are infinitely ambiguous.

Quantum consciousness potentially carries the formation of information of every phenomenon that can emerge during all these processes. What emerges is the product of the universal laws and constants. In other words, no matter what the process is, the information of what will happen in which process potentially exists. The issue of how that information will take shape cannot be predicted or foreseen on a scale of certainty before the process takes place.

If we call this entire operation the information itself, we can also say that everything consists of information. Consciousness is a current part of this information operation and depends on the stages and operation of the movement within the process. In other words, consciousness also potentially comprehends the entire information.

While we experience the interpretation here through our emotions and thoughts, iron powder experiences it through its sensitivity to the magnetic field, and the Earth through gravitation while rotating around the Sun.

Information and consciousness are infinite in size and the entire existence is a part of this system. Information and consciousness work as the active-passive forms of each other at the quantum level. In other words, if the origin of existence is energy, what tries to interpret it is consciousness.

At the same time, what we call energy is actually information and also potentially carries the consciousness within itself. Consciousness is not a phenomenon different from this information; it is a phenomenon that we evaluate as if it is a different thing even though it is a part of information.

What makes us perceive this differently is the dimension of movement (time). Without movement (time), this difference would not form and meaning would not emerge. For instance, as in the relationship of the transformation of potential energy into kinetic energy, energies are equal. However, we differentiate them and define and interpret them as two different energies.

On the quantum basis, the option that an object defines its own objectivity is only available through movement. In other words, the change a moment before and a moment after creates meaning and information movement and consciousness emerges.

If movement stops in the universe for a moment, none of us could understand what is happening to us, because time must pass (movement must continue) for us to understand what is happening. It is necessary that "time" passes for us to understand what happens between before and after.

The concept of a "moment" is the period between a second before and after within this movement. If it takes 24 hours for the Earth to turn on its own axis, as we do not know what this movement period is on the scale of cosmos, we cannot have information about the universe's own dimension of time. For us, the concept of "a moment in time" is our awareness process. In other words, it is the process of being aware of what we think. Time and movement are the active and passive forms of each other on the scale of quantum. In other words, it is an operation where one does not exist without the other, and even if it existed, it would have no meaning.

What is called meaning or awareness is a dimension that emerges with the existence of these two concepts. In other words, it is the common movement at the joining or separation point of information and consciousness.

Here, let's go back to that dark room and continue with what the other components of the event are. If you pay attention, we can say that there are actually three components at the heart of all of our definitions. The first component is the fact regarding whether the room and the phenomena in the room "exist" or not. It is necessary that if there are things in the room, those existing things are possible according to the universal laws.

The second component is the existence of light and the phenomenon that makes the light illuminate the room and make the things that exist in the room visible and recognisable (this phenomenon actually represents the operation of the universal laws).

The third component is the existence of a structure that realises, interprets and defines what happens (our consciousness) in the environment.

If one of these three components does not exist, a content integrity would not emerge in what exists in the room (this detection is only valid for our own reality and our own consciousness).

As we stated before, two realities and operations exist about whether or not we exist in the room.

In the first case, it is the fact that if the room exists, it exists as an operation and reality outside of our existence, regardless of whether we exist or not. For instance, the existence of a black hole in the centre of the galaxy is a reality independent from whether or not we are there. In other words, it is the fact that the universe has its own reality whether or not we exist in the universe.

The second phenomenon is the case that we are in the room and a part of that reality.

The fact that we are a part of a reality outside of us is the case that in addition to the universe's own reality, we are also a part of this reality.

It means, whether or not we exist, the universe always has its own information and consciousness reality anyway. This is because if this reality did not exist, we would not exist as a part of it anyway.

Our existence in the universe does not only mean we exist in the universe as a part of this information and consciousness operation of the universe. At the same time, we also have our own information and consciousness structure.

Existence of the room, the light, and the existence of a universal consciousness regarding what the things in the room are is a situation independent from our existence. This consciousness already includes the information of all events that occur in that room and in the universe. The case that we are in that room is the fact that we also participated in the room as a part of that universal consciousness that exists outside of us, and we understand and define that information.

Consequently, ours is a limited local information and consciousness. The other is the information and consciousness that includes us and all other things and covers the whole. We can see and understand the information and consciousness that includes the whole in the double slit experiment.

The electron that we will measure is a part of the information and consciousness of the universe because everything is connected according to the law of thermodynamics. The fact that we are there and perform a measurement is also a part of the universal consciousness. Just as we know the existence of a table and chair in a room, and if we look at the events with the logic that the universal consciousness knows that we are there and are making a measurement, we understand why the electron behaves differently.

This situation is similar to the logic and principles of tossing a coin. A coin has two sides and in accordance with the universal laws, you only see the side of the coin which you are looking at. This is because we can only see the side of the coin at which we are looking and cannot see the back side as we look unilaterally.

The probability that heads or tails comes up is the same at the moment you tossed the coin. Potentially, both heads and tails can come up.

However, again in accordance with the universal laws, either tails or heads must come up when the coin falls on the ground. This is because one side of the coin must face the ground due to gravity. The same principles of necessity determine that the electron behaves either in waves or as a particle.

When you make no measurements, the movement of the electron carries the characteristics of being both a wave and a particle, just as when you toss a coin. However, as you want to see a result, the electron has to behave either as a particle or a wave.

This is not surprising; on the contrary, it is the indicator of the fact that the universe has collective information and a consciousness network. Similarly, the entanglement law is also a part of this with similar principles. At the quantum information level, everything is connected, no space exists in the size of an electron, and everything is a part of this information. Even what you call space is also information and everything is a part of this. The operation of information and consciousness in the universe is an intertwined structure like darkness and light.

Think of the universe as the lamp in that dark room. If the lamp is turned off, everything is dark and undefined. (This is the same as the situation that an object cannot define its own objectivity or the situation of stability or singularity where no movement occurs.) Whenever the lamp is turned on (a movement occurs), everything becomes visible and gains a meaning.

When the lamp is turned on, although there is light, darkness does not disappear. Darkness still exists but you cannot see it. When the lamp is turned off, darkness appears but then you cannot mention the meaning of what you see in the light because everything is dark. These are the systems that depend on each other, bring each other into existence, and interpret each other.

If we define darkness as information in the universe, consciousness is like the light that illuminates it and gives meaning to it. These two are the phenomena that cannot be considered separately and are intertwined. You are unconscious when you are fast asleep. This is just as when you are in darkness. The moment you wake up, darkness disappears and everything finds a meaning like when the lamp is turned on.

3

PASSIVENESS OF THE CONSCIOUSNESS

Light is a part of its source before it leaves the source forming itself, and it is like the source. In other words, it is the state of the light source and the light itself being the same. In sum, it is the state of being "**we**". The moment the light leaves its source and breaks off, it then becomes itself – it turns into "**I**".

In fact, a similar event (active-passive disintegration) is experienced as the "moment" in our consciousness as well. What enables the knowledge continuity in our consciousness is the receptor stimuli and the memory basis. Our consciousness and the light structurally resemble each other in many respects. Light is formed passively as a result of the combination of nuclear fusion and the atoms in the star core. The light that exists passively in the star core is active for the whole of life when it comes into the world and it gives energy and life to all creatures. In other words, the light is both active and passive, and similarly, our consciousness is both active and passive.

While we see only one colour of the light, the light contains different colours, different energy levels, and different wavelengths within. Similarly, our consciousness structure includes five wavelengths, and it is both active and passive.

Humans have receptor sensors called "the five senses". Each of these five receptor stimuli represents a part of our active consciousness. Unlike the five stimuli, a sixth structure that is formed by the combination of those five stimuli in the same "moment" emerges. This emerging sixth structure both includes five receptor consciousnesses in itself, and it is a structure with its own characteristics unlike the five stimuli. This looks like the light contains all colours within and yet seems white. In other words, each colour has a feature and they create a new colour and feature when they combine.

This sixth consciousness is both a different consciousness from the five consciousnesses and it carries the features of the five consciousnesses, which includes a receptor infrastructure. In other words, it includes material and energy roots (their own software and consciousness). Because the sixth consciousness is formed as a result of a combination, it does not have an individual, private receptor root. In other words, it exists as a different consciousness but it does not have a material root because it does not have an individual receptor root. This means it does not have its own active structure and it exists as the passive of the five stimuli.

This case is both the activeness and the passiveness of the consciousness. If we could delaminate our consciousness just as we separate the light in the prism, we could see many things there about our past and future. The junction point where the five senses intersect is the point of our cognizance and consciousness. Our sixth passive consciousness formed by this intersection is our consciousness by which we are linked to the consciousness of the universe, and by which we are aware of ourselves and comprehend our existence. As a result, the moment we are aware of ourselves, just as the moment the light is noticed in complete darkness when it is formed, is the moment we notice the universe and that we are a part of the consciousness of the universe.

It is not very appropriate to define the difference between the universal consciousness and our consciousness. However, I would like to present a couple of examples to give an idea functionally and in terms of capacity. Let's think about the cinemas and computers available on the Earth's crust. Imagine that you went into the cinema, bought a ticket for the 3:00 p.m. matinee, and you are going to watch a romantic film. Well, which films will people be watching in other cinemas and computers all around the world at the same time? Some will be watching action and violence films, some will be watching drama films, and others will be watching biographies.

The session of the film you will watch will last for 120 minutes, a fiction fit into 120 minutes, and a narration formed by thousands of scenes. When you watch the film from the beginning to the end, an integration will be formed in your brain. You will watch the beginning and the end of a love adventure, and what you see there will constitute content integrity.

You will see the mistakes made or efforts exerted in this film. You will follow the cause and effect processes, and in the end you will complete the film with an end for which you will feel sorry or happy and return to your own life. What you will watch will match up with your life experiences and you will watch scenes that seem to explain what you have experienced before. Your consciousness in the film you will watch will be your consciousness for the last "120 minutes". This consciousness will be the blending of your experiences you have had until that "moment", and it will be a small period of your life in this world.

Now, let's take you to that cinema with a time machine and begin to show you around among the scenes of the films watched in other cinemas and computers around the world in that 120 minute session. In other words, let's show you around one film scene in one moment, and another scene in another moment, and in the end, together we will have watched 120 different film scenes in 120 different films.

Well, what will we have watched at the end of 120 minutes?

In this case, no content integrity will have been formed in the scenes we watched, and we will have watched 120 different scenes on 120 different topics. None of these scenes will have meaning and have formed a perception that will constitute our integrity of feelings.

Well, does it mean the scenes we cannot make sense of are really meaningless, or do the films make no sense to us although they are meaningful in themselves because we have only watched a short time frame?

Well, what is reality? Is the thing we call reality related to our finding something meaningful or not? Is it the things we perceive in watching a romance film in that cinema? Otherwise, is it thousands of events occurring outside of us and is it the elapsing film frames? Although we do not experience the events ourselves, where is the place of things experienced outside of us in our reality definition? Are the things experienced by others not reality because we do not experience them ourselves?

Now we can consider the creator consciousness a structure that lives, feels and comprehends all these life experiences at the same moment. In other words, we can regard it as a structure that experiences thousands of events and watches thousands of films at the same moment, and comprehends and makes sense of the theme integrity of all of them.

If we, as humans, watched 120 film scenes at the same moment, no content integrity would be formed in us. However, all these events and scenes are linked to each other in the quantum energy and consciousness level, and a consciousness that perceives the integrity itself is in question. The size and the capacity of this consciousness is not a structure that includes holiness, and it is an indispensable feature and consciousness dimension of the asset.

Watching and understanding our own film as a human, instead of watching 120 films at the same moment and not understanding anything, will be a more realistic and appropriate choice.

We can develop our own consciousness trying to understand this consciousness. However, trying to understand this consciousness itself would be an extremely improper and meaningless request and expectation. Therefore, be yourself and try to discover the beauty of being yourself. If you discover yourself, you will understand your own integrity without the integration itself and live your own integrity in the consciousness of the whole. And then you will also understand the whole.

If we regard our consciousness and existence on this basis, a determination like, "we are born as light and return as material" may seem meaningless to one person while it can be the bare truth for somebody else. For example, we cannot know who will watch which film in which cinema. No matter who watches which film, we eventually know that everybody is watching a film. **We know the reality that the scene we watched is our own film in the universe**. Therefore, be realistic and do not be mistaken by describing who watches what to people. Try to comprehend your own reality and deal with the reality of your own scene.

A person asks themself the following questions about **the meaning of life** in the scene of some people.

"Yes, I am here as "**me**" and suppose that I do not complain about anything. Well, why **am I not successful, or could not be successful?"**

"What did I do wrong to become unsuccessful?"

"Why did you allow me to make a mistake and did not prevent my mistake?"

As a result, this questioning persists until comprehending the fact that a so-called mistake or success cannot be a choice and these are an illusion.

Similarly, people can behave disrespectfully and selfishly as if they are taking revenge for coming into the world with the peevishness that "**now that I am in this world, I want money, power, and prestige,**" or suffer for longing with the loneliness that "**what mistake did I make so the Creator gave up on me and deprived me of himself?**"

All these perceptions are about how a human analyses life. However, no matter which perception you use while analysing life, life also has its own reality. Although your analysis is realistic and correct according to you, this situation does not mean that you have analysed life correctly. Therefore, we should not forget that everything cannot be as we see it.

4
CAUSALITY

If a phenomenon, existence, description, fiction, or analysis is mentioned, its causality should definitely be consistent or though not itself, at least its effects should be observable. Otherwise, we conclude that we should accept every lie or flight of imagination. In order to understand what is right or wrong in the analyses people put forward, especially about belief, specific methods and operating universal laws are required. People can believe in everything they want or wish, but they cannot expect us to believe in those things in the same way as well.

They cannot expect us to believe in the things they believe in with an approach such as "If I say it, I say the truth". In life, there are things that every person knows are right or wrong and believes in. What we believe in may not be important as long as it does not affect our relationships and life. However, in the case that the things we believe stir controversy between other people and ourselves, or result in negative outcomes in our life in any way, we should have an understanding of what we believe to be defensible and right.

Realisation of this opinion requires the presence of references by which we verify what we believe. These references should be common values that other people, apart from us, adopt and approve. So these values should be scientific and universal in order to be common references. For example, the majority of the community of a country can have a belief or they can have rights or wrongs according to their own belief values. However, if these rights do not comprise other beliefs or cannot be values for others, we cannot say these values you believe in are universal and they are common references. Therefore, it is indispensable for our reference values to be universal and scientific. We already see that a belief and opinion should be of a common mind and conscience and be scientific.

The aim here should be to think what is reasonable and logical, to speak a common language and to resolve problems rather than just learn what people think. and why. After all, if this does not become the aim, it will not be important who thinks what or why they think it. With the questioning and the determinations we do, we will have understood and learnt the infrastructure truths of the points of which maybe we have never thought before. Perhaps we will have understood our own reality.

To be able to find the correct answers to the questions in our mind, we should do the following determinations first. This is because we cannot find the answers of the claims put forward without making these determinations and taking them as references.

1) First, a cause should definitely form a result (action-reaction law). The result formed can be a cause of something else but can never be itself. This is because a change is definitely compulsory and if nothing changes, it means nothing happens. However, even the things that seem unchanging change in the quantum energy level and we know that a change is in question. If there is a change, then a concept of **time** must be available. If there is a change, we cannot regard any phenomenon as if it would not change, and **there can be nothing in the universe that will not change or transform (except laws and principles). This is because they are already those that perform the change.**

2) An object cannot automatically form, change, and define its own objectivity. In other words, the world cannot automatically form itself. Under these circumstances, if there is a formation, it also obliges the presence of two structures: a structure that exists and a structure that makes existence. Because of this obligation, there cannot be an "absolute singularity". This is because if there were an absolute singularity, the universe would not already exist, and therefore, we also would not exist. At this point, the so-called singularity should have at least two components or it should move at least two components. This is called "the unity of contrasts", and these are not necessarily in contrast. We name the obligation of the presence of these two components as the **law of symmetry**. Presence of a structure that triggers the power to perform the Big Bang is compulsory in order for the Big Bang to occur. Just this requirement of "**other things to occur**" in order for "**some things to occur**" is the principle of **necessity**. Questioning this formation **after it is realised** is the principle of **causality**.

3) If the laws of symmetry and necessity did not exist, the concept of **dimension** would not come into existence and everything would be meaningless. In this case, our perception system would not exist. This would be as meaningless as your defining yourself in a non-existing world with your non-existing existence. Thus, the existence of a concept of dimension necessitates the existence of specific laws. As required by these laws, a structure equivalent to the universe in exchange for everything before and after the universe should exist. In other words, if the universe is to reoccur it will occur from the present universe again.

4) If a motion or transformation is in question, the progress of this transformation process with every moment, in other words, the existence of a speed of motion necessitates the law of **active-passive**. Events that occur between one "moment" before

and after the transformation refer to the cognizance moment of our consciousness.

5) All material and energy structures in the universe that we know or not, function **on the necessity basis**. Moreover, what we call causality is trying to understand the reason for the events resulting from necessity. From the **active-passive** perspective, what is active is "necessity" and what is passive is "causality". This is because "causality" is the operation of consciousness' questioning the events and trying to understand them. In the universe we live, "the consciousness questioning causality" is passive because it is formed after the existence of the body and the formation of the brain. Every necessity has a causality and every causality has a necessity. They cannot be separated from each other (as our brain and consciousness cannot be separated from each other). This is because both of them are the symmetry and necessity of each other at the same time.

If a movement is in question instead of a formation or transformation, formations occurring based on this movement are defined based on the law of active and passive in the same way. As in the example of magnetism occurring in the poles while the world is rotating, what is active is the Earth, and what is passive is the magnetism occurring depending on the rotation of the Earth. The existence of a passive form necessitates an active form, and the existence of an active form necessitates a passive form. Here the function is not reversed and the magnetism cannot form the Earth. Only the Earth can form the magnetism.

SCIENCE AND RELIGION IN CAUSALITY

Beliefs try to embrace many concepts that belong to humanity such as morals, fairness and justice as if they were concepts belonging to God. Because these concepts are based on consciousness, they are perceived as if they are the topic of beliefs rather than science. In fact, these concepts that are known as the equivalents of rights and wrongs in human consciousness should not be simplified to any belief. The concepts in question are the functioning form of the laws of the universe.

What is called belief is actually consciousness, the topic of science and a phenomenon that can be explained with science. Both structures, science and belief, that have been tried to be separated try to explain life and existence, and the origin of both is again consciousness itself.

On the other hand, there is no taboo in science, and understanding that testing and verifying each idea put forward is essential. Science is different from religions in this aspect. **The perspective of science is based on an analysis from the active form to the passive form, while the analysis of beliefs is based on an operation from the passive form to the active form.** Instead of the concepts of good and bad in science, the concepts of possibility and impossibility in the operating laws of the universe are in question. Therefore, the concepts of good and bad are actually the results of laws operating in the universe.

In science, the consistency of the cause and effect relationship, and the operation of movement and balance laws, and energy are important. This operation is perceived and defined as good or bad in our consciousness system. In this context, ideas and theories are not taboos and no holiness can be attributed to them.

The moment the mistakes and wrongs of a theory are observed in a scientific approach, this theory is revised and updated making definitions suitable for new data. The principle that everything is changeable and transformable has already been accepted as a law from the beginning. Therefore, nothing is absolute and unchangeable in a scientific approach. In belief systems, on the other hand, what is explained is considered absolute and unchangeable as they are based on God.

The concepts of belief, put forward thousands of years ago, regarding the creation of humanity and defining humanity and existence are like the invalid science theories of today **(refer to the reverse operation from the passive form to the active form).** This is because the things that are put forward have no scientific equivalence and proof, and many explained narratives are against the laws of science and natural operation. Because there was no possibility to verify the inaccuracy of them in the past, the concepts in question remain today. However, today we now know more clearly what can and cannot happen.

Today, we have the opportunity to evaluate and observe the opinions put forward in the past based on more healthy foundations thanks to technological knowledge. Today, the basic point that science and beliefs differ from each other is the causality arguments related to the existence of the universe and humans, and whether these arguments can be possible, or not.

Beliefs explain a creation legend in their own way. Regarding the reality and the proof of what is explained, the argument "**God has adequate power to do everything**" is presented as data**. If you pay attention, this understanding defines the law of necessity as the power of God.** Beliefs state, in their way, the fact that necessity does not require causality as an understanding that God can realize existence without needing a reason. In fact, an explanation about the existence of a formation should be consistent and realistic on a scientific and belief-related basis.

Attributing the unknown or unexplained events to God is to take the easy way out and disregard the facts. This is because if you attribute the unknown things to the acceptance of God, you block the questioning and comfort yourself in this acceptance.

If no reality and consistency is sought, it will not be important who believes in what and what they accept in any case.

In order to better comprehend the topics about science's operation on a scientific basis, let's try to understand why we think and evaluate these topics in a different way from each other and find the answers to our questions together. In other words, let's try to understand the operation of arguments about the presence or absence of God on a scientific basis.

The starting point results from the request for existence to be described and to be based on an excuse.

An analysis of what the structure or power that brings this universe and us into existence is with the logical proposition, "if the universe and we exist, an existing structure should definitely have a structure that brings it into existence" is the point that distinguishes science from belief.

The fact is that it is never possible for someone to know who this power or structure that brings everything into existence is, and how to define it. This is because a structure that exists in the universe cannot have knowledge outside the universe. Although we will learn how the universe came into existence, we will never learn on what grounds the universe exists (we will never know the intention of the Creator).

Here, the so-called belief is people asserting that they know what this excuse and God's intention are (their assertion that they know God's excuse on why he created humans). People assert that they know this excuse through the argument that the creator power selected a person as his messenger and explained to this messenger why he created the universe and humans.

However, nobody can prove that these arguments are right. This is because even if God himself came and said, "This is what the right thing is," you would have no way of knowing that he is God and what he said is right (this is because you can in no way verify whether the entity giving the information is God himself, or not).

Because you cannot be sure that what was said is true, you prefer to just believe, or you look on with suspicion and pretend to believe. What you believe will not be the things of which you know and you will be sure of the truth itself, but it will be a **belief** of the assumption and **acceptance** that what was said, is true. There is an acceptance-based belief similar to this in the origin of all beliefs. If these acceptances cannot be verified, they are not the truths themselves under any circumstances, and they cannot be true.

This is because an acceptance can be true only if it is verifiable and observable. The laws and principles of the universe already tell us that these acceptances cannot be verified and possible. **Even thinking that what is said can be possible, is ignoring the universe's law and principles.** This is because this case is like a case where you can regard a glass hanging in the air without it falling as possible and believing and defending it even if you know there is gravity. Or it is convincing yourself based on the assumption that "yes, there is gravity" but maybe there can be an exception and someone can do this. Or convince yourself with the assumption that "if beliefs say this, it should certainly be a reality".

No matter which excuse is put forward, none of them are technically real and cannot be possible. **This is because a creator power or consciousness is not an existence that would talk to people, explain an excuse to them, or verify the excuses people**

put forward. Even the opinion that the Creator speaks to people is an unrealistic, presumptive acceptance. Nobody can say that this is true, and nobody can prove this.

If the Creator has a language and speaks to you, you should know that this language is science and the laws of the universe. If we are to understand the structure and consciousness that create us or bring us into existence, we can understand and explain this only in operation and principles. This is because these laws and principles already belong to the Creator and the laws of the universe are his laws. Isn't ignoring the laws of the universe when they do not serve our purpose also ignoring the Creator? This is because if God created us and he is as beliefs have explained, then is it not God who created the laws and principles of the universe?

When these laws say that something is wrong, to what extent is it sincere, persuasive, ethical, and rational to keep ourselves above these laws, and assert that we are telling the truth? How sincere a behaviour is it to defend laws when it serves our purpose, or verifies us – or to deny the laws of the universe, or make an explanation for the operation of them in our own way, producing possibilities when it is contrary to our expressions? If we want scales to weigh light for us and heavy for others, while weighing something, it becomes not the problem of the scales but our intention, aim, insincerity, and inconsistency of using the scales.

I know that there are some people who wonder whether it would be disrespectful to God if we had a doubt about the existence of God, or about our belief. What you should doubt is not the existence of a creator. This is because if we exist today, there is, of course, a structure that brings this creature into existence. However, what you should have doubts about are the things beliefs explain to you about what the Creator is, and the definition and understanding of the Creator in their own way.

Then ask yourself this question: how, and from whom, do you know that your doubts are disrespectful to God, or not? How does the person who says this, know, and what is the source of this information? How realistic is it if the majority says that these assumptions are true and you convince yourself that this is true? Who will you believe in when others tell you that these assumptions are not real? It does not mean that something will be right if the majority finds it right – history is full of examples about this. They, and you, know very well, you can never be sure that what is said will be true.

A person's belief in an acceptance, even though they do not know or are not sure of it, is the origin of the belief.

Belief in a truth itself, and that an acceptance is real, are not the same things.

Here, the difference between them is the difference between science and belief.

Our acceptances bind our world together and they are individual. In fact, truths bind everybody together. If we regard our acceptance as real and expect all humanity to accept this, we make a mistake and impose on others our acceptance as if it were real.

It is actually what beliefs try to do. Therefore, no reality is in question in these acceptances of beliefs, instead, "**slyly defining the unknowability in their own way**" is the question, and the arguments beliefs present on that what they define are real are actually incorrect legends.

We can again understand from the scientific principles that the reason for creation can never be known. Because the scientific perspective knows this truth, it deals with the creation itself instead of looking for a reason for creation. This is because looking for a reason for creation is an action that you cannot get a result from. Because causality comes after necessity in scientific terms, a person who follows a path in accordance with a way of scientific thought knows that they should deal with the period after necessity instead of before, and they do not try to deceive themselves. They take the period after the Big Bang instead of the period before it as base. This is because there is nothing to do or change for the period before the Big Bang. In other words, they are sincere in what they do or do not know, and defend the truth without even bothering to be sly. They prefer to access the final information they can access and explain the truth based on this information instead of believing in an acceptance in their own way. Humanity will learn how the universe came into existence in due course in any case. However, humanity will have answered the question, "How did we come into existence?" being aware of, knowing, and accepting the fact that they will never be able to know the reason for creation and the intention of the Creator, even if they learn how the universe came into existence.

In fact, what concerns us is not the answer to the question "Why?" Instead, it is the answer to the question, "How?" This is because whatever the reason for existence is, it is now a topic that we can object to and change. If we are looking for a reason to satisfy ourselves, we can find an infinite number of "reasons" and believe in them.

However, we can still never learn which one of them is the real intention of the Creator. Maybe we came into existence due to one reason, or maybe due to many reasons. Maybe science and scientists will have found thousands of reasons until that final stage. They will find each of these reasons not as a reason based on an acceptance but as reasons existing in their own operation of science and the laws of the universe, and everything they find will be verifiable and real information.

Also, defence mechanisms and psychological reasons lie behind people's belief in the existence of non-existing, impossible, or unrealistic events. **The basic mistakes of beliefs are ignoring reality and the laws of the universe, and in spite of them, presuming and believing that something will happen.**

If you ignore the laws of the universe, then you can convince yourself of the mistake that everything you think of will exist or is real. However, if you ignore the reference that something can happen or not, it means that you believe in the probability that everything is possible and drift away from reality. This is also a state where a person is lost and dispersed in terms of consciousness. This is because when references that determine reality and the imagination, or right and wrong disappear, you begin to fall apart since you will have lost your will about which event you should evaluate, how you evaluate it, and where you should put this event.

Although we are not aware, this psychological reality and dispersion exists in the origin of belief. **People choose to believe in an acceptance as it is easy due to the difficulty of dealing with an uncertainty and coping with it (it is usually not a preference made consciously).** For example, when we lose a very much beloved, close relative, it is very difficult to accept this loss. To cope with this pain, we choose to convince ourselves that they will be greeted in good conditions and be happy in heaven, although we have lost them in this world. We hope that there is heaven for our beloved ones, wish that it really exists and want to believe in this. This is because we want the best of everything for our beloved ones and find peace imagining that they are in good places.

This case is not a choice we made consciously but a defence shield our defence mechanisms generated for the purpose of consolation. We console ourselves, relax, and wish them to be true by believing in them. If someone happens to say that they are not real, we consider the expression of these people as an attack on our source of consolation, and we become uncomfortable feeling that we have been accused of deceiving ourselves. We think that these people are disrespectful towards our beliefs.

This is just like the psychological state a child experiences when he is dispossessed of his toy. However, the problem is our acceptance of the facts and wishing to face them. This is because the possibility that these people are saying the truth will mean that we are dispossessed of our source of consolation, which will disturb us.

We live the anger of it when we are dispossessed of our source of consolation, and we feel helpless and incapable. We all experienced this feeling when we were a child, and all of us know this feeling. When a child wants something that will make them happy, they are not interested in the reality of it. They do not question why they want this and whether the thing they want is possible or reasonable. Even if what they want is not reasonable, they are not interested in why it cannot be possible and want combatively only this thing to happen.

We consider this behaviour of the child as brattiness and know the fact that the conditions are disregarded. We think that the child will understand this when it is time to and we try to console them. In fact, this combating child is still living inside all of us and still directs us, although not as it used to.

The radical defenders of the beliefs are individuals who could not get rid of the effect of this childhood psychology. This is because these people are individuals who have convinced themselves of, or are conditioned to believe that, what they think and believe is real without questioning the facts. Because these individuals are conditioned to think that what they believe in is "real", they are stuck on the point of why other people do not see or accept this fact. In other words, they accuse other people of not seeing the fact without realising their own conditioned state.

However, it is themselves who do not see the fact, and what they believe in is not the fact itself but the **acceptance** they have convinced themselves of, and they are not aware of it.

Yet, it is not the same thing to believe in a fact and suppose that what they believe in is real. No matter if we are aware or not, there is always reality and it will eventually be understood. What is a problem here is in which process we can comprehend this reality or not. As long as we postpone seeing reality, we lose so much time on behalf of humanity.

The answer to the question "Why is reality important?" is the point people have come to today. The origin of all hunger, poverty, war, injustices, and tears is directly related to the non-comprehension of these realities.

The fact of correctly understanding and comprehending people lies behind the origin of the respect towards other humans and nature, the bond between all living and inanimate entities and their responsibilities.

The point of what this bond is, is a case whereby we can see and realise being completely realistic. In other words, being an "upright" person is not a preference, but a necessity and the sooner we realise this truth, the sooner we become "human" and find a way to live in peace.

Well, why does the difference in question occur, and why does a person reject something someone else finds right? I wonder what the actual correct thing is.

In fact, such difference in approaches is a necessity and has a scientific base.

Such contrasting approaches result from the law called "the law of symmetry". According to this, it is concluded that everything has two appearances: opposites, or completers. It is an indispensable structure like the existence of two sides of a medallion.

In other words, it is distinguishing between the understanding of explaining the unknowability based on an acceptance and the understanding of accepting the unknowability itself and trying to understand or learn it. For example, a human consciousness can have an approach to God such as, "**I should exist, so I think of God and make him exist.** As it is me, I think that God exists and makes him exist" while another consciousness can have a contrary approach such as **"God should exist, so he made me exist".** If God did not exist, what made me exist would also not exist. Therefore, I would not exist and would not know the existence of God.

Well, what if creation or existence did not exist at all? In other words, what if we did not exist at all and had not heard about anything?

While putting this option on the table, we encounter the question **"Well, why has creation or existence occurred and why do we exist?"** This question is the basic, inevitable question of the causality of existence. In other words, asking why we exist if we exist, is actually an inevitable and compulsory question. In addition to this question, we encounter the question, "Does the reason for our existence depend on causality or necessity?" In other words, what is the cause and effect relationship and the purpose of our existence?

It is an important topic, whether our existence depends on a necessity or a causality and which one of them comes first. This is because it is important which one of causality and necessity is active, or which of them is passive, in terms of the operation of activeness and passiveness (whether we believe in an acceptance or follow the fact itself).

If we exist, then we should think that "**we had to exist so we existed.**"

If we exist in spite of the option of not existing at all, there should definitely be a necessity in our existence. This is because even if there is a reason for our existence, there should be a necessity for the requirement that there should also be a "reason" for this reason (an infinite chain of "reasons" for "reason"). In fact, you cannot clarify your existence with any "why" question. There will be a "why" question for every argument you will put forward, and you will see that you are obliged to be attached to a necessity.

Furthermore, a person who does not exist at present will not ask the question, "Why do I exist?" This means, even to ask the question, "Why do I exist?", first, there must be a necessity of a person's existence. In other words, a person should mandatorily exist and only after that can they ask the question, "Why do I exist?"

And because of this necessity, if we exist, we can see that there is a **necessity** before a causality in any case. In other words, the principle and law of necessity comes first in all formations in the universe we live in and this is an active structure. The causality comes after necessity, and it questions and exemplifies the necessity – causality is the passiveness of necessity. This is because causality is a question of consciousness. The consciousness itself is already passive and it existed afterwards. Causality and necessity are the inseparable symmetry of one another. The universe has been experiencing a change and transformation process since the "moment" of the Big Bang. Therefore, the "time"-dependent course of this process necessitates existence and operation of the law of "**active-passive**".

Here we can say that we can understand the response to the question about the consciousness of God from the operation and principles of this active-passive law. The most basic characteristic of the active-passive law in the change and transformation process is **the passive operation of the material and the energy or the law of the universe for the events or formations which occurred in the past as of the "moment", and the active operation of them for the events and formations which will occur in the future.** In other words, the formation of the solar system and the formation of the Earth after the Big Bang are passive structures which occurred after the Big Bang. The Earth's rotation around its axis and the magnetism which occurred at its poles is a passive structure which occurred after the formation of the world. In other words, a passive structure is not a structure that brings itself into existence and forms itself.

We can also regard the issue in the same way on scientific and belief bases. The scientific community asserts that existence begins with the Big Bang and tries to understand why and how it happened. In other words, it tries to analyse the events following the active-passive sequence. Religions and belief systems do not content themselves with this. They move their own passive consciousness until the time before the Big Bang and attribute existence to the creation idea of the consciousness of God.

If there is a consciousness today, there was, of course, a consciousness before the Big Bang. However, **it is insincere and sly to make a conclusion that** "If there was a consciousness before the Big Bang, then this consciousness has created and formed the universe as we said."

Nobody can know what the consciousness that makes the universe exists is, and nobody can defend that they have talked to this consciousness or received messages from it. This is because you cannot consider the universe's consciousness to be like your own consciousness. If there are approximately 8 billion people in the world, you cannot consider the universe's consciousness as an entity like you, just as you cannot consider all these people as a single person.

This means the effort of the entity that existed afterwards to get ahead of the entity that made it exist. In other words, it is trying to do a reverse analysis from the active state to the passive state. **However, this analysis is the mistake of reverse operation of universal laws. This is because it means the existence definition (the idea that God created the universe as thinking) is made by us after the universe and we existed.**

In other words, it is the understanding of the period before the Big Bang by us, who existed in a passive form billions of years after the Big Bang, with our own passive consciousness. Here the error or the mistake is that the passive structure indirectly ignores the active structure and tries to assign its own passive consciousness as an active consciousness.

For example, we, as a passive structure (we who existed after the universe came into existence), consider "the idea that the power that thinks of, and creates everything, is God" as a solution by thinking as if we were active and were obliged to find a reason for our existence. In other words, we make sense of our reason for existence with the idea that the Creator brought the universe into existence for humanity with the purpose of specifically creating humans. In sum, we believe in the idea that God created the universe just to create humans and "he created us privately".

In this idea of "being privately created", there is also the enthusiasm and effort of thinking themselves superior to other entities. In other words, this is the effort of us, who exist as an "**effect**" in the cause and effect relationship, to assign our own consciousness as a "**cause**". In other words, it is like the magnetism that exists passively in the poles of the world, believing that it is created for the world to make its own existence in order to make its own formation meaningful.

In fact, the existence of the world and its own objectivity is not for creating magnetism specifically. In other words, the aim of the existence of the world is not just to create magnetism. The existence of magnetism is not active. It is passive and a natural result of the objective existence of the world. A similar structure and operation is also valid for our consciousness.

What is active in the creation of consciousness is our brain – it is our material structure. In this line, the consciousness that "**God should exist so he created us**" is the passive consciousness of us that existed afterwards. If our body and brain did not exist, this consciousness of us would not exist at all. We cannot think of them separately from each other and do analysis. **Therefore, it will already be inevitable for us to think that there is a power that created us if we exist. However, thinking of that is not an explanation of why we were created. The information for why we exist is the information that can be understood in the own information of the structure and process that made us exist and in the universal principles that operate in us. Existence of information and operation, and our understanding and making sense of it cannot be separated from one another.**

Here, in the case of the existence of one of them, the inevitable requirement of the other is the principle of necessity of symmetry. The simultaneous existence of both cases is a necessity principle of the activeness-passiveness law. This is because the so-called consciousness is already both an active and a passive structure. Therefore, we can think of both of them.

You cannot separate these structures from each other as required by both symmetry and activeness-passiveness laws in the essence. You cannot alone say that "something is correct".

Here, what we call "**consciousness**" is actually the simultaneous existence of both our "**creating**" and "being **created**" consciousness as of the "moment". In other words, it is the state of both being active and passive. This means, "**No matter for which reason we exist, we will mandatorily question the reason for our existence**". We cannot separate and consider individually the thought **"I exist, so I think of God and make him exist"** from **"God should exist, so I exist."**

Let's try to better understand the operation by giving an example from our existence. Let's question the analyses of beliefs of our birth and the reason for our existence, and evaluate the consistency of these analyses together.

If we regard our own birth from the cause and effect relationship perspective, our existence will be an effect. Again, if we regard our own birth from the cause and effect perspective, we will see that we are passive structures. The active structures are our mother and father, and we are the passive structures coming into existence from them.

These cannot be operated reversely and separated from each other. You trying to operate them reversely or separately means that you are trying to operate the laws of the universe reversely. You cannot reversely operate the laws of the universe as the material and the energy system. For example, you cannot reversely operate gravity. However, you can make an assumption that the laws of the universe will operate reversely on the consciousness basis. The results you will achieve as assumptions by neglecting the laws of the universe will still be results that are not in accordance with the laws of the universe, and they will not work. In short, if you think of a formation that neglects gravity, this formation will be erroneous and cause trouble, and will not work.

When we regard the events considering the analyses as belief systems doing by ignoring many things, let's try to understand together how things will be confused.

According to the analyses of beliefs, "it is God, who created us and gave us life and spirit". As a result, now that we exist, then what is the meaning of mother and father who brought us into existence. **Now that we exist, then were our father and mother mandatorily created and brought together just for our birth? In other words, were "we obliged to be born" and were our mother and father created and came together just because they were obliged to bring us to the world? In other words, did our mother and father come into the world as two unimportant figurants that were brought together by God just to bring us into the world?**

In the scope of another probability, did our mother and father come together naturally and we come into existence? Now that we have been born, then was God obliged to give us life and a spirit just because we were born?

As can be seen from here, when we try to bring our own existence forward and make it active, denying the reason for the existence of our mother and father, although we are passive compared to them, we reach a non-logical conclusion such as everything in the universe was created for a person to be created. In sum, we conclude that it seems like all the universe was brought into existence just for the creation of a person, and this is a mistake.

This mistake is ignoring the reverse operation of the laws of the universe or the active-passive sequence. The laws of symmetry and the active-passive relationship are generally ignored in the analyses of beliefs. The fact that they are a whole and cannot be separated from each other is disregarded. This state means reducing the existence or the creation to just one option (one of the active or passive forms) and ignoring the other option. However, if our mother and father did not exist, we would not exist. If we exist, then the necessity of the existence of our mother and father cannot be separated from each other and they cannot be thought of individually. You cannot take one of them as active and ignore the passive form, or take the passive form as active and define the actual active form according to the passive form.

As can be seen from here, when we try to assign ourselves as active, although we are passive, contradictions occur because the system cannot operate reversely, and it is understood that we are not active. The analyses of beliefs about existence and life are incorrect because of this mistake, and they are full of contradictions.

EXISTENCE AND CONSCIOUSNESS IN CAUSALITY

If we comprehend that we exist, then this existence should have a foundational operation. This means we have a physical existence, a matter/energy structure, and a consciousness that comprehends this existence. The fact that from where, how, and why our consciousness and matter structure have come into existence has been reflected upon throughout the history of humanity.

In fact, the whole picture has not been understood because it has been looked at from two different sides of symmetry throughout the history of humanity. In other words, a fight has been made about "Which came first, the chicken or the egg?" and the truth that they cannot be separated has always been ignored. Thus, the entire story of existence has actually been based on two scenarios.

The first scenario predicts that creation or existence cannot depend on the will of a creator, and if there is such a will, evidence should be provided for it. The other scenario is based on the existence of a consciousness of God that thinks and creates everything that exists in the universe including matter, energy, and consciousness.

Because this issue dates back to the beginning of the history of humanity, we cannot address it in depth; however, together we will analyse the truth that both scenarios are deficient and inconsistent.

Materialism is more consistent than idealism because it is based on nature's dialectics. In addition, we can say that new analyses are attempted through the combination of them today. However you try to analyse the issue, no non-scientific analysis will be correct. Therefore, we will discuss the issue together on a scientific basis and try to review the conflicts of these analyses through scientific references.

Because belief systems base existence on a consciousness of God before the Big Bang, we will start our review from the period before the Big Bang. According to the argument of beliefs, God wanted to create the universe and humans before the Big Bang, gave the order "Be" for everything to come into existence, and the universe began to emerge.

As the justification of this creation, arguments such as the fact that humans who worship God, are virtuous, and are worthy servants to Him are made. We will analyse God's justifications to create the universe and humankind but first we should **structurally** analyse existence on the basis of matter, energy, and consciousness in terms of certain principles.

The "moment" when God said, "Be," according to beliefs, corresponds to the "moment" of the Big Bang on a scientific basis. Accordingly, there is an analysis that "God had always existed before the Big Bang and created us out of nothing because He is almighty, and thus, the universe was created".

Because such scenarios also include the period before the Big Bang, we cannot present them as scientific data. However, we know that things cannot appear out of nothing or disappear from existence according to the existing law of thermodynamics. In other words, if the universe and consciousness exist today, there should be a power or structure that corresponds to today's universe before the Big Bang.

As humanity cannot know what this structure was before the Big Bang, it is called "nothing". According to the creation scenario of beliefs, God created us out of nothing. According to this scenario, we are in a dimension separate from God as we were created. In other words, this means we live in the created universe, and God, who created us, exists in another system or dimension outside the universe.

In summary, there are two separate dimensions and systems. We are in one of them, and God, who created us, is in the other.

In fact, this fiction of beliefs is a model of the universe from thousands of years ago. Today, there are also many models of universes such as parallel universes or multiple universes within the scope of scientific analysis. The difference between them is that beliefs add the "consciousness of creator" to the model of the universe and provide reference to the fact that as the power that created the universe, the consciousness of God has the power to do this (in other words, they are based on acceptance).

We already principally know that if there is a consciousness in the universe we live in, there would be a consciousness in the structure before the Big Bang, too. However, existence of a consciousness before the Big Bang will not mean beliefs' analysis is a correct analysis, and the acceptances are not correct acceptances.

This is because the existence and operation depends on the universal laws and their operation as we explained above. Belief systems use obscurity with masterful craftiness and market their own analyses to humanity as real information and the solution for obscurity.

As we cannot provide data on the scientific basis for the events before the Big Bang, people can still believe whatever they want to believe. However, if we search for the truth, no analysis other than science is realistic or correct.

Whatever you believe happened before the Big Bang, we cannot believe whatever serves our purpose and make an analysis of the events that have occurred after the Big Bang, because despite the universal laws, we cannot defend the correctness or reality of the analyses we will make. The reason for this is that creation or existence already occurred and the process operates according to the universal laws.

Whether creation or existence occurred through God's order "Be" or if it came into being by itself, it **requires** everything that has been created to comply with the laws of creation or existence. In other words, even if creation was made by a God, as beliefs define it, it requires all "created" things to obey this order of creation. Thus, after creation, universal laws must operate anyway. The fact that beliefs attribute the events that occur "today" to the consciousness of God before the Big Bang is an effort to reversely operate the working laws of existence (the fact that passive defines active according to itself). While on the one hand it is told that those laws were created by God to carry out God's order "Be," on the other hand, it is defended that God disregarded these laws and interfered in the operation. In other words, beliefs defend the arguments, which mean God is not sure what he is doing and interferes in, and makes corrections on, the laws he created and which conflict with each other, as the miracles of God.

While on the one hand it is said that God created the universe and humans by calculating everything in advance, on the other hand, it seems like it is defended that God makes mistakes and interferes in the operation to fix these mistakes.

The reason for these conflicts is the thought that the Creator is different from these created things. In other words, the said conflicts stem from the mistake that the Creator is a phenomenon different from what he created. In this case, the fact that the structure that created existence cannot be a phenomenon different from what exists, could not be understood, and this truth has been missed. In other words, the reality of creating from itself, not out of nothing, could not be understood.

The biggest mistake is the mistake of separating the "Creator and created" from each other. These are structurally the same things; and they are operationally separated. We can also call this the active-passive operation.

If you make the analysis in this structurally mistaken way in the first place, you will analyse every event depending on it incorrectly, anyway. The same conflicts are also maintained about the operation of the universe and the justifications for its creation, in addition to the conflict in the structural analysis of beliefs. We see these conflicts in every area of life and explaining them one-by-one is a separate subject of analysis. Therefore, we will be content with making only certain questions.

For example, there is a conflict in the justification regarding the fact that God gives consciousness and spirit to humans. If God gives consciousness to humans and humans question God, then normally, this should not be deemed a crime and there should be no punishment for that, because if a servant of God questions God, they question with the consciousness God gave them. If God does not want to be questioned, he should not have given that consciousness to humankind, or should have given a consciousness that would not question him.

Religions do not find this kind of questioning true and evaluate it as disbelief.

There should not be a case where God gives humankind a questioning consciousness and then uses a contradictory expression like "Why do you question me?" If our questioning is a problem, then would it not be more consistent that such a consciousness was never given to us?

If God created good and bad, then with what justification will he punish his servants who are not satisfied? If consciousness is something given to humans later in terms of the operation of the universe, then why is the consciousness of humans who lived a thousand years ago different from the consciousness of now?

If God is "absolute" and gives consciousness to humans later, why then were humans who lived a thousand years ago not given the consciousness and knowledge that we have today? This is because if what we call consciousness is an absolute structure given by God, independent of matter, energy, and the evolutionary process, then it should also be a standard structure independent of evolution and time.

While on the one hand beliefs do not accept the evolutionary process, on the other hand, they unwittingly conflict with their own argument by defending that consciousness is given depending on the evolutionary process. However, we know that our consciousness is a structure that develops depending on our own evolutionary process. The consciousness of humans who will live a thousand years from now will be more improved than our consciousness; and those people will be more knowledgeable than us.

Another conflict is among the justifications regarding the creation of humans. When humans come into the world, they are not asked whether or not they will come into the world or whether or not they want this. Moreover, if a person came into the world as a person who is subjected to injustice by everyone, why would God ask that person to always do the right thing and be patient, despite that? Does this not mean that God discriminates against his servants and is merciless, or that he plays with his servants like toys?

If God created humans for good purposes, then why does he make things difficult for them by creating evil in the world, too? With what justification does he ask humans to be servants worthy of God despite all the evil? What are the crimes of the servants to live an injustice where one sleeps hungry while other sleeps full? While it is said that God is fair and compassionate, why do some people always suffer, and others inflict cruelty and live in prosperity? While you are asked to always be an honest, fair, and merciful person, why are those who do not obey this allowed to do so? What are the crimes of the people who suffer from this situation and where will these people seek their rights? Whom will they call to account for the difficulties they have, and what is God's understanding of fairness? Most importantly, who needs all this chaos?

If God created humans for the justifications that beliefs set forth, would it not be more consistent that they were never created and did not ever live them instead of living through all these injustices and conflicts?

Humans did not come into the world by bargaining with God about heaven or hell. If they were asked whether they preferred not being created instead of being created with these justifications, perhaps no one would want to live through all these. To what extent are the explanations such as "You are not able to understand these things. God knows something and will absolutely reward humans" sincere, consistent, convincing and reasonable?

If we look at the subject from a little technical perspective to solidify these justifications and analyses of beliefs, we will better understand the subject. For example, you built a robot factory, produced a thousand robots with the same hardware, and installed a specific software in all of them. You installed in only one of the robots the software regarding what they should do to survive without hurting each other and let all the robots out into nature. So, what will be the crimes of the other robots, who do not exactly know what to do?

How will the other robots know which robot you gave the required information? When every robot says that they have the required correct information, how will they understand and know what the correct information is and who has it?

Will the robot to whom you gave the required information really stick to the information you gave it, or will it make some additions or omissions?

If it does not work and the robots still hurt themselves and each other, then will you install the software in a new robot and send it?

Some will believe that the new robot tells the truth and some will not, and will you send another robot again?

When we look at this scenario from a technical perspective, we see that this chaos is not necessary at all. If you place a chip for information transfer in every robot, you can transfer what you want to transfer directly to all robots.

If we can make this analysis with our human mind, is it not weird that God did not do this? As far as we understand, these analyses mean beliefs' effort to underestimate God's mind, because on the one hand, you will say that God creates everything thinkingly and knowingly, and on the other hand, you will be in conflict with your own justifications in these scenarios and try to attribute it to God. **As can be seen, the actual problem is not whether or not there is a creator consciousness of God, or whether or not God created humans.**

The problem is the conflicting analysis about what these creator consciousness of God and acceptances are. If you call the power that created everything, God, of course there is a creator structure and consciousness that brought the universe into existence or created it. However, existence of this consciousness does not mean what beliefs say is true. What beliefs try to do is to define the real Creator structure according to themselves.

For example, every living person knows that their parents who brought them into existence exist, and there should be a structure that brings everything into existence. However, suggesting that "if all these exist, what created them is God, and God is like we say he is," is to impose their own God on humanity.

The logic of the suggestion being followed is an irrelevant logic of suggestion such as "**Cyprus is an island, England is also an island, and thus, alligators are green,**" and this is a wrong suggestion. Perhaps all these analyses were required and necessary analyses in the past. However, the fact that humanity still cannot distinguish between them after all these years is a grievous situation for humanity. This is because the reflections of these analyses are just like the harmful side effects of a drug. There are effects that separate humanity from sincerity, responsibility, and its own nature.

People have been made passive, used, and exploited with the arguments of beliefs. Correcting them is important and required for the future of humanity. For example, similar to the robot scenario, they believe that they are always defective and imperfect like those ignorant robots and see themselves as inadequate. This is because they question and come to the conclusion that "I must be imperfect and defective, so God is not close to me, does not give me the required information, and guide me," and find themselves excluded, inadequate and defective. What beliefs impose on people is the option of "Do you want to die by means of forty mules or by means of forty cleavers?" In other words, it is an imposition that if you say there is a "God," you either will accept an understanding of God as we explain, or you will not accept the existence of God.

This understanding is the imposition that "If you say there is a God that created us, that God is a God as we define it. If you do not accept God as we define it, it means you deny yourselves and God."

However, the creator power does not have to be a power like people say. In essence, the fact that people make such a definition is not a situation that is in compliance with the operating universal laws and principles. This is because we are not even the microscopic pieces of the power that created the universe and our consciousness cannot have the capacity to define everything.

Even if a definition is made one day, right now we are far away from making this definition.

Today, the fact that we try to define the power that created the universe can be nothing short of an effort to create a new religion. Therefore, instead of defining what the creator power is, it will be a more correct and realistic approach to define what it is not.

As can be seen, the justifications that are told to us, saying that beliefs come from God, are full of conflicts. **The effort of beliefs to define the Creator is technically the mistake that the passive structure defines the active structure.** At the utmost, these are people's own acceptances and arguments that they produce themselves with reference to God and are unrealistic.

Although beliefs emerged for good purposes in the past, and analyses of beliefs were made in good faith, people have used beliefs for bad purposes such as exploiting people and keeping them under control throughout history. Beliefs have tried to keep humanity in line with these justifications, but these justifications have brought blood and tears instead of peace and happiness. Fights over beliefs have been made, and blood has been shed throughout history up until this century. Today, the arguments of beliefs include justifications that restrict humans from seeking their rights and being free individuals. So, what is the reason for beliefs' reign for all these years?

The reason for this is that what beliefs defend do not have proof, and that people want to buy peace believing the beliefs' promise of heaven. Another reason is people's motive of finding solace in the understanding of a God that will call people to account for injustices when people have become incapable of fighting against injustices, as well as the dominance of the sense of belonging in herd psychology.

What is promised belongs to the post-mortem and are the things that no one can prove. These promises are the fictions and acceptances that are told with the comfort and craftiness of knowing the truth that humans will not come back after they die. If someone does not believe and objects to what is said, they are asked to prove it themselves. However, today we have a better comprehension of what is impossible in the operation of the universe and nature compared to the past. If what is told were true, it should comply with the universal laws and we should obtain self-verifying results in all cross examinations. Most importantly, the justifications should not conflict with the causality of fiction. If you provide justifications like it is a blessing that you have been created as humans, and set forth conflicts that mean you are God's toys, then you lead people to chaos. With the most basic conclusion, if almost the entire world population still lives in hunger, tears and injustice today, it is an indication of the fact that there is a problem in the fiction.

If these justifications and fictions were correct and consistent, should all these negativities and injustices not be at the minimum level? Creation did not occur how beliefs tell us based on their own acceptances. "God" is not a power that is separate from us, and created us out of nothing – he is a power that is with us every "moment" and created us from **himself**.

We are already his parts with either our matter structure or our consciousness structure. Just like the fact that billions of cells in our bodies are our parts, we are parts of the creator structure as well. Living or nonliving, we all come into existence from the same place. We, humans, have come to life for a short time and live in a process called a lifetime like everything in the universe. At the end of this process, we will transform and continue to be a part of the consciousness in the universe. Right now, we are humans and experience the human consciousness. If you are wondering what kind of a consciousness we will have after we die, let it be a surprise from the consciousness of the universe to us.

Instead of living with the concerns regarding heaven or hell on the other side, try to live what you want on this side. Live with dignity and fairness, keeping in mind that everyone has the right to live just as much as you do. If you manage to live in a way worthy of a human, you can be sure that you will already deserve to live in the place called "heaven" that beliefs have promised to you.

Today, people who see the conflicts of religions set forth with a large number of reasonless ideas that we can call new movements of religion. There are many movements such as nirvanaism, clairvoyant, Galaxism, etc., and they completely confuse people.

In fact, these movements are not much different from the religions, which people deny. They are also after selling people other dreams and hopes. None of them are realistic and based on science. Thus, NO ways, methods and definitions that do not overlap with science or go along with science can be correct.

Master Seyyid Nesimî gave very clear answers to people's enthusiasm to define the Creator centuries ago in his work "Two worlds fit into me".

Two worlds fit into me, I cannot fit into this world

Two worlds fit into me, I cannot fit in this world
I am a homeless ore, I cannot fit in any place

The universe is my evidence, my beginning goes back to the person
Recognize me from this sign but know that I cannot fit in the sign

No one has known the God with doubt and suspicion
Some may know the God, and I cannot fit in doubt and suspicion

Look at the semblance and know the real meaning in the semblance
I am both the body and the spirit but I can fit in neither the body nor the spirit

Seyyid Nesimî

The essence of what is tried to be explained in this work is that a definition of God cannot be made. If all the living or non-living structures that exist in the universe come together and try to make a definition that the power that brought us into existence (creator power, God) is "like this" or "like that," right at the "moment" when you form an opinion, by bringing trillions of characteristics and probabilities that may or may not come to mind, you cannot make any definitions, because it is intended to be said "Know that the Creator is not that, either".

Thus, let's understand why we cannot define the Creator. We, as the granules of a whole, cannot comprehend and define what the whole is. Otherwise, it would be an improper definition like the fact that a cell in your body tries to define who you are. Thus, such a definition is reasonless and is against the law of the instrument.

What is important and necessary here is not the definition of what the Creator is or will be. What is important is the fact that you define yourself correctly, and your bond and connection with the Creator. If we exist, it means we have a physical structure, a matter and energy structure, and a consciousness. All of these are the parts of the Creator in us. Our consciousness of existence is our connection with the creator universe consciousness. This structure is like how a mobile phone detects and connects to the GSM station when it is turned on.

In addition, our matter and cell structure, which is not reflected in our cognisance, also has a subatomic quantum consciousness.

This consciousness hardware exists in all living and non-living creatures' own objectivity and does not need us to define it.

Thus, it would be more accurate to look at and evaluate this in terms of understanding and interpreting rather than with the logic of defining. **When we follow the principles of causality to understand the consciousness in the universe and ask the questions "what is the consciousness of "consciousness" or can consciousness experience its own consciousness?" we know that this experience cannot occur. This is because we are stuck on the fact that an object cannot define its own objectivity (the necessity of the law of symmetry).**

Consciousness requires the existence of a formation other than itself to experience itself. These are the fundamental laws of symmetry and necessity. Consciousness can experience itself only over the existence of that formation. For this reason, the universe has a matter and energy dimension and the laws and principles of transformation. Consciousness experiences itself over this matter-energy structure.

For example, our experience of the world through our senses (smelling a flower) creates a definition in our consciousness. For instance, smelling a flower is our consciousness' experience of matter. **We can also consider the creation of this consciousness that we experience, as a system that operates in the way that the creator consciousness in the universe also experiences our consciousness.** At the same time, this also means the "consciousness of the universe" experiences our consciousness. We can also think that the entire existence in the universe and the operating system is a part of this very experience. This definition is valid for our human consciousness. We can also see that the universe has another consciousness structure that is outside of us and that we do not experience. We know that a consciousness, which has carried out the evolution in the transformation of the process from the Big Bang to today, exists. However, we could not experience this entire process as consciousness.

The atoms and elements in our bodies may have broken off and come from hundreds and thousands of stars and taken shape in our bodies, however, we do not remember or know any of this. From which processes we have come until today in terms of consciousness is a subject that science is already working on today and may be solved in the future. However, the process after that is more important for us because the answer to the question, what kind of a future we will build, will be the product of our current consciousness. Our current consciousness is active for the future and is in our hands.

Just like our transition from carriages to automobiles, tomorrow's happy future will be the product of our current rational consciousness. This is a process, and it means humanity will continue to suffer and be unhappy every lost day. This is also a waste of time for humanity. For example, if humanity took rationalism as a guide, and belief systems did not corrupt people, perhaps we would be born as happier people and living in a world that could be called "heaven".

When we turn to the causality of consciousness, the part that concerns us is actually obvious and clear. For whatever reason we exist, in the end, we currently exist and are living in a world that exists. Other people and living creatures also live together with us. If we can see the whole where all humans and all other living creatures live, and if we can comprehend the consciousness that the Earth is our home and the other formations are our siblings, then we will be "humans" and become aware of our responsibility.

No one who achieves this consciousness can pass the buck or try to put their irresponsibility on someone else. Above all, they cannot be insincere and act in laziness and hypocrisy saying that "everything comes from God and he makes us do everything – so, what is my crime?"

Of course we all are special as individuals. However, considering the entirety of humanity, we all are the same as parts of a whole and we know that the same system operates in all of us. Whatever a person means when saying "I," it cannot be something that belongs to themselves because this person's body and consciousness already belongs to this universe and they are the audience in this universe.

No one acquired their own body and consciousness on their own. They came to life in a body as a part of a process and are the active-passive structures of that body as a consciousness. What gets hungry, gets thirsty, and suffers is the body, and what they call "myself" is what experiences this. When someone does an injustice to them, what gets upset about that injustice is the operation of the references that operate in the consciousness of the universe. The feeling that an injustice is done is the reference and reasoning of that consciousness of the Creator. When they do an injustice to someone, what feels remorse in them is the conscience of the Creator which operates in themselves.

Every person carries both themselves and the Creator's voice, conscience and consciousness, and references of fairness inside themselves. This structure is our connection with the consciousness that created the universe and our experience is also its experience in us. If people think what they think only belongs to them, they are mistaken, as the structure in them is the same structure that everyone hears and feels and that is in everyone. As the people who know this could not correctly explain this operation or could not be understood correctly due to the period when they lived, the issue has gone up to irrelevant definitions.

For example, the saying "God is everywhere, in every moment" is essentially true. However, if you then describe God as a sacred entity different from you, it means you do not know the meaning of what you say. Yes, the Creator is everywhere, in every moment, because everything is already a part of it and emerged from it. In other words, living or nonliving, everything and all of us are the parts of that creator structure both before and after the Big Bang. The creator structure is not a different structure outside of our existence and consciousness, living or nonliving.

Of course, when we say this, a question like, "How can a tree represent God?" can be asked. There may be people who do not want to accept this. However, the truth is that the tree is also a part of God with its matter structure and aliveness. Here, the main reason why humans revere God is based on the fear of death and the infrastructure of their disappearance and the bereaving of their consciousness. People tend to ingratiate oneself with God and wait for a special behaviour toward themselves by revering God. At the same time, people are in an effort and arrogance of seeing themselves superior to other creatures. This understanding of the holiness of beliefs is about their expectations from the concept of God. Beliefs are based on the understanding of seeing God as an almighty creature and seeing themselves as incapable and helpless creatures because they discriminate between the Creator and the created.

Because there is "an unapproachable difference between humans and their creator" according to this understanding, people always suppress themselves with the understanding that they are inadequate and incompetent. According to this suppression, there is an understanding that God does not connect with humans because "it is like humans are creatures that do not deserve their humanity and that are not worthy of God".

The people who assume that this understanding is correct believe that God is indifferent to them "because they are always defective and guilty". The justification of the fact that humans are called "servants" at the heart of religions' creation arguments is already based on the understanding that "humans are inadequate". On the other hand, the conflict that humans are superior to other creatures is given along with this understanding. Neither justifications of beliefs, which conflict with themselves in line with both understandings, are correct.

However, we have no differences from other living creatures. Our only difference is that we have the consciousness that the Creator exists and is our consciousness of being aware of him. Having consciousness makes us neither servants nor the most distinguished creatures of the universe. The fact that we are intelligent creatures is both a privilege and a responsibility.

If you address the issue only from the dimension of privilege and ignore responsibility, this seems like giving a machine gun to a monkey and letting it out on the streets. This means what makes humans "humans" is not their intelligence, it is their sincerity and consciousness of responsibility.

Emergence of this consciousness is possible by seeing the big picture. When we see the big picture, we grasp the truth that no one is a separate structure from you, that we are a family, and that we are all siblings.

We should not forget the fact that we are actually the same in order to bear the responsibility of the consciousness of being a human. Do unto others as you would have them do unto you; do not deem it proper for them. If you want to love, learn to be loved, and if you want to be respected, learn to respect.

WHAT IS HOLINESS IN CAUSALITY?

A person's understanding of holiness, in other words, their deeming something holy, is caused by not understanding themselves correctly. The following understanding lies behind the holiness: "I am an inadequate and passive asset, therefore I am in need of, and grateful for, the active structure that makes me exist." However, on the other hand, as being the passive form of the active form, you cannot separate from it and you are already an indispensable result of the active structure.

In fact, in line with the understanding above, you skip the fact that the asset you deem holy will have no meaning without you, and you and the asset you deem holy cannot be thought of differently from each other. In other words, how holy the asset you bless is, means you are as holy as it. This is because what makes the asset you bless holy is your considering it holy. In fact, it is a relative concept, and the foundation of both social and individual holiness is based on acceptance. Therefore, not precise accuracy can be mentioned for this acceptance.

"If it is God who makes us do things and it is us who does them," then what is our responsibility and crime?

"If it is us who makes us do things and who does them," then where is God, and what is the meaning of saying, "God causes everything to be done?"

"If it is God who makes us do things and who does them," then who are we and of whom and what are we representative of?

"If it is God who says, and it is us who do not obey," then where is the power of God's sanction?

"If it is us who do although God did not say," then why do we lay the blame on God?

Who gave this idea of "creation" to God, **who created everything?** What is the necessity of him to create in this way?

Does not **"the all-powerful God"** have sufficient power to create a better humanity?

If people believe in a God and deem their belief holy, then they should first know the answers of the questions above. If it is said, "Yes, I believe in God but do not know the responses to these questions, and I do not necessarily know these responses – only God knows the responses to them," then it is an insincere line of questioning. This means taking the easy way out and even being disturbed by people who question those who do not take the easy way out because they do not think simply like themselves.

If people **call the power that brought us into existence, God,** there should, of course, be a power that realises existence.

Otherwise, we would not be present here. However, if there is this power, making an inference such as, "What we say is true, and there is a God as we define it" is also an insincere approach. The power that brought the universe and us into existence has already been in existence since before the start of the universe. This power brought everything into existence by transforming itself into everything that exists. This transformation still continues and will turn into other formations in the future. According to the analysis of beliefs, God is a power that only does good. It is said that the other power that creates evil is the Devil. If the Devil acts out of the will of God, then we cannot say that there is a single creating power. If the Devil acts depending on the will of God, then why is the Devil accused? How sincere is it to try to attribute the occurrence of bad things to the Devil? Doesn't God have sufficient power to not allow the Devil to bother people? If he allows it, then what is the crime of the human? If God is all-powerful, there will be neither crime nor sin when he annihilates the Devil. What is the crime of the human that he is a toy of God and the Devil?

If there is a test, how fair is this test? If God creates a person, the will of this person is weak and the Devil deceives them, then why didn't God create that person with a stronger will? What is the fault of a person who was created with a weak will to fail this test, and what is its measure of justice? Moreover, these religious definitions of God are based upon there being no living creature in the universe other than humans. If there are thinking creatures in the universe other than us, will their definition of God be the same as ours? Therefore, how accurate and realistic is it to make definitions about God and the universe as if we are the only rulers of the universe?

The aim of the forced analyses here is the search for the answer to the question why **"good-bad"** contrasts exist in the world. These are analyses for the questioning of why nice and good things do not alone dominate the world. However, what we call "good" and "bad" are requirements of the laws of symmetry and necessity. This is the reflection of the energy system operating in the universe as **"good-bad"** concepts to our consciousness. It is the perception of energy, at one end of the symmetry, as "bad" since it causes us discomfort, and the perception of energy on the other side as "good".

The system works to balance energy at both sides. This point of balance is our state of being neutral that we call "satisfaction". In fact, everything we do in life is composed of our effort to establish this balance. If you gradually release water from a dam into a field, plants in the field are revived and we perceive this as a good thing. However, this time, when you unblock the dam and release water into the field, water will bring destruction rather than revival to the field, and we perceive this as a bad thing. Here, our consciousness system works just as the case of the water from the dam, and we perceive and define the events or stimuli as good or bad.

GOOD-BAD:

What is called bad is a universal perception and since all humanity uses the same references, what seems to one person as "bad" is actually what it seems to all of humanity.

The universal definition of badness is "something that is done to you that you do not find right".

The universal principle of goodness is "the requirement that you should not do unto others as you would not want done unto you".

A bad person is a person who is egocentric and perceives and considers an event only according to themselves, without considering the rights and feelings of the other party.

In other words, this is a person who does the thing that they say is bad when it is done to them; but who believes that they have the right to do it and who does not feel responsible for it.

Apart from the contradictory doctrines specified by beliefs, the insincerity of the so-called believers make everything twice as contradictory. To better comprehend the issue and to be able to compare these doctrines and determine which of them are correct, it is necessary to correctly explain some concepts and know their real equivalents and meanings. These concepts related to people's beliefs are the concepts of "having faith, believing, knowing, loving, being sincere, and having merit". We can understand how sincere people are in their beliefs from these principles. There are principal and functional differences between believing and having faith.

Believing: Is a feeling that does not have a concrete equivalence in your cognizance and that you cannot experience.

(You believe in God, but you do not have the chance to experience it.)

Knowing: Is a feeling that has a concrete equivalence in the cognizance and that can be experienced.

(You know that there is gravity because you can experience its existence.)

Having faith: Is the meaning and feeling you attribute to the thing you do not know, but believe.

I will not give further details of these since their infrastructure relationships and principles depend on technical solutions. However,

I would like to address the relationship between "loving, having faith, merit, and belief" with a short example to understand this relationship.

The infrastructure of a sincere person to have faith depends on a perception of commitment for which you can say, **"even if you leave me, I will never leave you."** (Origin of commitment of love.) In other words, it is the destiny of "I will never give you up, no matter where I live." The people who really believe and have faith feel that bond with the Creator. People can feel a similar commitment for their beloved ones without realising it. However, the thing to which attention should be paid is the requirement that it should be mutual if you love a person with such a bond.

If the person you love does not share the same feelings for you, you perceive it as an attack against your beliefs, faith, love, and personality; and experience the feeling as if you had been left by the Creator. When you cannot find an equivalence in your commitment to God, you cannot think of accusing God. In this case, you should do the same thing for your beloved ones.

One of the commitment indications is the understanding of deserving love based on fairness – the other is worship. However, neither God nor your beloved ones need your worship. This is because people who fail to be worthy, fair, and sincere choose to worship because they are deprived of these characteristics and try to fill their deficiency by worship.

A similar contradictory operation can be very clearly observed in every part of life, for example, between the wealthy and poor. Poor people try to eliminate the discomfort of economic deficiency through the promises of beliefs. Rich people, on the other hand, try to eliminate the discomfort caused by injustice through so-called help and "goodness".

If a person really loves God or their beloved ones, they try to deserve their love. They never consider the accusation, "I love you, why do not you love me **as I love you?**" suits them. This is because having respect for the beloved one and deserving them is in question in one case, and the understanding of self-justification and calling the beloved one to account is in question in the other case. Therefore, many people regard themselves as believing and faithful without knowing the origin of love and commitment. However, there is sincerity in the origin of having faith and love, as there is in everything. It is impossible for a person who does not know sincerity, to know what love or faith is.

The perspective of the bigotry of belief on the events and logic of their evaluation is based on these same incorrect propositions. This is just as insincere as the players of an amateur neighbourhood team questioning why they are not playing in the championship league **although they are a football team,** and their defence of that discrimination is made against them. These people even make the accusation, **"Why do you not think simply as we do and become like us?"** instead of seeing their own deficiencies. Unless the contradictions of their own ways of thinking are explained to these people, they will continue to boast about themselves and regard others inadequate with the negligence of believing in their own rightfulness.

First of all, relying on such people means a person's insincerity against themselves rather than respect of their belief. This is because in the case that such people are reinforced with herd mentality, they will neither question themselves, nor make progress in the name of humanity. If beliefs and religions could have developed humanity, there would not be hungry and desperate people today, and peace would be dominant in the world.

The other infrastructure reality of the bigotry of belief is some people's belief in their own sect leaders on behalf of a belief in

God. People are so insincere about a belief that they can exhibit all kinds of slyness under the appearance of "I believe the most". On the one hand, these people deem being a toady of the sect leaders they consider belief leaders, as the indication of believing. On the other hand, they defend that their belief is at a point over the belief position of their guiding leader in case this leader is faulty.

A person who thinks like this hides behind the assumption that "I do not make mistakes. The mistake must have been made by the sect leader," and hopes that there are some people whom they will accuse in the case they are faulty – they calculate the cheekiness of being able to say, "I have been deceived," when required. Since the aim or intention of such a person is something other than believing in God, doing what is told by the sect leader rather than "God" serves their purpose more (in other words, they suppose they behaved slyly). Thus, they find it more advantageous to do the things said by the sect leader rather than by God, whom they claim to believe in.

Yes, we cannot know now what every living person on Earth thinks and what calculations they make. However, we know what will happen to humanity if a meteor as big as Canada hits the world. We do not know how much money, faith, or belief people have but we can know that these will not matter after that meteor hits. We cannot know what people will take into consideration and what they would give up for money and power, and what they would sacrifice in exchange for them, but we can know that their money will not be useful when they continue with the same mentality and there will not be a world in which to spend this money.

I am sure that those who say they believe also see and know what we see, but in spite of this, they pretend not to see these things. What is harsh is that these people believe them to be normal and fail to be disturbed by contradictions and feel responsible for them; otherwise, they are disturbed by people who question them.

People have such grief and say, "I wish I had not been born at all and I had not had such experiences," being so incapable, helpless, and tearing their heart out – and unfortunately people live this grief. People transform into something else to be able to breathe when they experience such grief, and they lose their faith.

Another misery is the fear of being deprived of the beauty of the world which is felt by people who achieve everything they want. No matter which option is true for a person, what will be their answer when you ask the question, "were the things that you wanted to do worthy of what you lived?"

Is a human pleased with what they did with their life and themselves? A living person supposes themselves special as long as they live and they believe that the Creator will treat them, though not everyone, specially. Well, now that we come into the world for a short time and all these are experienced, then how should we live and what should we do?

The answer to this question is, of course, a person's being himself and living in a way that suits him. Well, what does a person's being themselves and living in a way that suits them mean?

A person's being themselves does not mean their doing and living whatever comes to their mind. **Being themselves is having a conscience on the basis of sincerity and responsibility and living in a fair way without trying to deceive themselves and others.** It is living knowing that a piece of your humanity is destroyed in every injustice you do. It is not doing what you do for an expectation of a medal – bribery for heaven, or fear of hell. A person's living with these targets is already making a deal with the Devil and selling their soul to him. However, being a human means being as valuable as not being bargained for.

The understanding of a bigoted person is they convince themselves that they are more intelligent and different than others. It is the slyness of believing that the Creator created them specially to hide their arrogance because they see themselves as different from, and superior to, other creatures. Therefore, they need a creator by whom they can convince themselves that the Creator created them to be different and special. For this reason, they feel grateful for the Creator and worship him. A virtuous person does not see this difference as superiority and arrogance. If there is a privilege and virtue of being human, they try to be worthy of this privilege. For this reason, the test of a virtuous person is not with God; it is with themselves.

If a human sees themselves superior to other living creatures, a forced conclusion, as if being human or being created as a human was a natural right of a human, and the Creator had to create "this person" as human is drawn. Yet, a person's being worthy of the Creator and their behaving in a way that suits themselves means regarding all creatures as works of the Creator, and loving creatures because of the Creator. Therefore, Yunus Emre said, **"I love the created for the Creator's sake".** Seeing being different in this way as a privilege, entitlement of tactlessness of being disrespectful towards everything by seeing it as a natural right, and getting out of the human attribute by losing the virtue of behaving in a way that suits humans, are the unlimitedness and arrogance of humanity.

The person who does not know the world of unity,
remains an animal in the shape of a human being.

Edip Harabi

When we question the causality of the human, we should seek the answer to "Why can't a human be more like a human?" instead of "Why is a human 'human'?" No matter, it is the Creator, and he created people in this way, and humans exist as a result of the development of nature – a virtuous person has the determination and responsibility of doing the right thing in every condition. This determination can be expressed as an understanding of being fair in everything.

"Does or should a person want what they think they deserve, or the best about themselves?"

This is a critical question. This is because a person can also ask, "Why am I obliged to make this choice?" The questions such as **"Why should I make this choice?"** or "Why is the thing I think I deserve and I wish for also not best for me?" are maybe the questions that a person should answer themselves.

However, if the things you think you deserve are the things that you were not able to experience, you should know that there are also bad things that you have not experienced. I cannot know how realistic or worthy a complaint it is to wish something by selecting the good things and rejecting the bad. Instead of complaining whenever you are obliged to experience bad things, or having to always stake a claim for good things, wishing the best for yourself is probably the most tolerable option (of course, this case should not mean keeping quiet against injustices).

Asking a question like "Others have that thing or this thing, so why don't I have it?" resembles the question of "Why am I not a tree?" They should believe that you are already "you" because the things that should have been done could not have been done to be the things that are thought as **"I wish I were so."**

The causality of your being "you."

"You" are already you because you need to be so.

"You" are you because you need to actually be this.

You are valuable because you are you in this way.

If you suffer because of being "you", you should know that you are on the right track and you suffer because you understand that something is missing.

If you are already pleased with your situation and yourself, it means that you do not know the reality of justice and fairness. This is because in this case it means you live the mistake of believing that you are complete.

Yes, it is a fact that we need to feel the idea that we are complete as a human. However, we cannot keep the fact that it is not permanent and absolute out of our mind or ignore it. This is because if we think that we are complete and our happiness is permanent, it means that we break away from our own realism and become selfish.

Therefore, we should not turn away from justice and fairness. You should not keep quiet and wait to be worthy of humanity; instead, you should do your duty towards the people who need you. You must always carry the fairness scales on your shoulders and in your conscience so as not to wrongly accuse somebody – and you must not remain insensitive to those who are in need. For example, even a bowl of water that you put on the street in summer is your responsibility to a living being. A human is a human only to the extent that they are sincere and responsible.

CAUSALITY IN NATURE

Wild thorns in Africa are plants loved by giraffes. To prevent giraffes from eating the leaves of this plant, it secretes a chemical called "grain" just before the leaves of this plant are annihilated.

The grain chemical embitters the taste of the leaves of the plant and transforms the taste of the plant to a taste giraffes do not like. This action is also carried out by the other trees in the savannah. Secretion of this chemical enables giraffes to go to other areas for food.

Now the most basic question is as follows:

How do these wild thorns communicate with each other?

The other questions are as follows:

Now that wild thorns know that giraffes will not eat leaves when grain is secreted, then why don't they secrete this chemical from the very beginning and allow giraffes to be fed with the leaves? Why do wild thorns withdraw the grain chemical from the leaves and allow the giraffes to be fed again when their leaves grow?

There are thousands of examples like this in nature. I will not address this topic very much because they are known. You can see the existence of an operating consciousness network in the ecological system. When you observe the universe and nature in an unprejudiced way, you actually understand the connection of everything to each other and see the big picture.

5

THE PRINCIPLE OF FAIRNESS

Fairness is a principal concept based on consciousness and represents the balance in the operation of the universal laws (it is actually the principle that we can call the causality of the law of necessity).

For instance, this principle is the conceptual necessity of the operation that determines at which degree the temperature of a glass of water will be balanced when hot and cold water is mixed. In other words, it is the principle of creation or existence which ensures the existence of even a single atom in the universe without being ignored and which protects that atom.

Fairness is principally the reason for the existence and operation of the law of thermodynamics, as well as other laws. This principle is the only concept that will not change and transform.

We cannot define what kind of a power the Creator is, but we can at least understand the balances and genius of the creator power a little by trying to explain and define the concept of fairness.

If you define something in the universe as sacred, you can define the principle of fairness as the holy grail of the universe. This is because fairness is the most fundamental principle of the concepts of sincerity, responsibility, morals, justice, and equity of humanity. Together, we will continue to explain the necessity of this principle within the subjects and will understand why this is an indispensable principle.

The evaluation sensitivity of fairness is at a level of weighing even the "shadow". The answer regarding what fairness involves an infinite times infinite number of probabilities and possibilities. Whatever is humans' consciousness phenomenon on the basis of consciousness, the conscious phenomenon of the consciousness of the universe is the principle of fairness. In other words, this is the principle of necessity of the operation of being equivalent, equal and balanced.

In fact, the system that operates our conscious hardware is already this principle. Just like you cannot define the Creator, you cannot define what fairness is. In other words, in terms of consciousness, you cannot define what fairness is; you can only define what it will be.

The principle of fairness is the ultimate limit that human consciousness can reach. If you try to define fairness, you make a "JUDGEMENT". In other words, you put yourself into the place of the Creator by expressing that you know the infinite uncertainty regarding existence.

Thus, the principle of fairness is like a curtain that determines the difference between our consciousness and the creator universe consciousness and that we cannot pass (because we are not the universe itself; we are part of it). In other words, fairness is a curtain which is impossible for us to pass even if we want to.

Whoever says that they pass this curtain (those who say that they receive messages from God, or say that they know the future, or speak for God), this is intentional speech, and they should be disregarded.

You can consider the existence of this curtain just like the necessity of a transformer that reduces high voltage to an appropriate voltage for the electrical appliances we use in our houses to work. This transformer is a structure that is required for reducing the energy to a level at which the appliances can work. Absence of this transformer means a radio that normally works on 12 volts would work on 300,000 volts. No radios work on this voltage, and any radio that says, "I received 1000 volts of electricity from the transformer, and I can work on this voltage" is not realistic.

This means "The transformer exploded, I received extra current, and I kept working on 1000 volts of electricity." If such things were possible, then we wouldn't need all of these universal laws and any of the information produced. Then let's all of us explode our transformers and enjoy the world!

Even though such speeches find buyers, such things are impossible. If there are trillions of universal laws, the meaning of these speeches is to ignore all of these trillions of universal laws.

Fairness also determines your position and status according to the creator's consciousness. No matter with what justification the Creator created humans or for what reasons humans came into existence, the mechanism that controls the justification of existence is again the principle of fairness.

The principle of fairness is the most fundamental principle, where the arguments of belief related to God's justifications to create humans will be questioned because none of the belief systems clearly defend that God is unfair. However, we can best see and understand that beliefs unwittingly conflict with their own arguments through the principle of fairness. The most fundamental principle, where beliefs will face the speeches they make for God, is the principle of fairness.

Let's review together and see how beliefs unwittingly interpret God's understanding of fairness according to the arguments of each belief. First, let's act upon principles and ask the question, "Why did God create humans?"

If God created humans for his own aims and wishes, with what rights did he do this?

Because humans' wishes were not asked, and their consent was not obtained.

Because created humans face injustices, and an unfair life is in question. Because God violates his servants' rights, because he created them without obtaining their consent.

If God created humans arbitrarily, what is God's understanding of fairness? The principle of fairness does not give the right to act arbitrarily and do an injustice to anyone, not even to the Creator.

Otherwise, the principle of **fairness** does not mean anything, and it would be God denying himself. This is because if the Creator considers they have the right to act arbitrarily because of his greatness, fairness cannot be mentioned. If fairness does not exist, then God's greatness and justice cannot be mentioned either.

This is because making a human, who came into the world and is suffering, this does not comply with God's understanding of greatness and injustice. This is because the human who is aggrieved has the right to victimhood.

Beliefs ignore this conflict by promising humans heaven. However, offering the bribe of heaven to humans as the compensation of this right does not comply with fairness. This is because delayed "justice" is not justice and does not comply with fairness. This is because you cannot be expected to ignore and be patient while cruelty is inflicted on you and you are suffering – this cannot be associated with fairness. If what beliefs say is true, then why have beliefs themselves not been patient and made wars and taken lives? Now that beliefs think they have the right to ask others to do something they cannot do, or to advise this to them, then to what extent are these speeches consistent and sincere?

Moreover, if a "servant" of God asks God the following according to the arguments of beliefs, what would beliefs' answers be?

"If I am a defective servant, then you must be to blame."

"Because you must be to blame, as you created a defective servant like me."

"If you created such a defective servant, then what can "my" crime be?"

As can be seen, the arguments allegedly produced to glorify God conflict with themselves and actually accuse God of being unconscientious and unfair, and of acting arbitrarily.

In principle, even if we are no match for the Creator, we should be his equal in rights and fairness. This is because it is not a principle that operates depending on greatness or smallness. No one can defend that the Creator will have the right to be unfair because he is great. Defending this also means defending that the Creator is an arrogant power that acts arbitrarily. This is because defending this is not glorifying the Creator but accusing him of being unfair and arrogant.

What will be understood from these arguments are conflicts of the enthusiasm of beliefs in defining the Creator. If beliefs could define what human is instead of their enthusiasm to define the Creator, they would probably do something more useful for humanity and humanity would be somewhere different.

This is because we are humans and being a human is an invaluable and exceptional situation. Those who are not content with either do not know what humanity is, or live in a world of dreams that they created in their minds, away from reality. In any case, both of them mean a lost lifetime.

People in this situation are so unconfident that they are afraid they will either become wild and go back to their cantankerousness in the period of caves, or feel lost without a belief in a God in their mind.

Do not fear my friends! If you are an "upright" person, you will be as happy, virtuous, and free as no beliefs can provide to you. This is because there are thousands of examples of people in the world who have managed to be an "upright" man and have lived as "upright" people without looking to God from the perspective of beliefs.

The criterion to be a human is not a phenomenon that depends on beliefs' justifications because being moral, virtuous, sincere and responsible are not concepts that depend on religion. If you see these values as required by "beliefs," you have not yet understood what humanity is anyway, because these concepts are not the concepts that beliefs invented but are the laws and principles that operate in you.

Now, let's try to understand how the principle of fairness operates in our daily lives and the roles of the universal laws in this operation. Actually, we are not aware of this operation because these laws work in our hardware. However, we can interfere in this operation and change it when we learn how it works.

First, we will understand the operation by giving examples of how the laws operate, then we will comprehend how we will affect the operation. If we define "how" humans think and "what" they do:

We can say that humans think based on quantum laws but live according to Newton's laws. In other words, we can think of the option of "**both this and that**" as the possibility that a two-option event occurs. However, it is impossible for both of what we think to occur. Instead, there is an option of "**either this or that**".

This operation is actually the principal operation of the concept of fairness. In other words, fairness has a single choice and a single result: It is either a fair result or not.

Depending on this operation, we blame ourselves for what we did or could not do in the past, saying that "I wish" I had done it like this. However, whatever your choice was in the past, you made that choice because that was the choice you should have selected at that "moment".

You think you had a chance to choose the other and you chose the wrong one. But thinking like this is a mistake. In other words, whatever you think, you will have the right to make only one choice and you cannot know which one is correct.

You will think that you did the right thing if what you hoped for comes true, and you will think that you did the wrong thing if what you hoped for does not come true. Presence of these two options in everything you will experience is a requirement of the law of symmetry. The presence of the good-bad distinction in every one of our choices is an operation that we cannot change. Humans' perception system tends to always choose the good one. This is because defence mechanisms do not want what is called "bad" to occur as they do not want to deal with the consequences of what is bad, and these mechanisms are programmed to protect you.

We need the principle of fairness for this conflict between good and bad to be tolerable. In other words, this is the law required for us to bear the consequences when what we call bad happens, and not to get spoiled and to lose and deceive ourselves when what we call "good" happens. This law is about making a choice or a decision without prejudice and making a judgement. In other words, it is a choice that you make without mistakenly being pretty sure about your choice. This is because if you make a mistake in a choice or a judgement that you will make overconfident, then you will face a huge discomfort.

We need the principle of fairness not to face this discomfort. We should be of the opinion that we make our decisions justly and fairly, not to feel uncomfortable with the consequences of our decisions. We, humans, cannot know whether our decisions are right or wrong when we make a choice or a decision; we make decisions without being sure of them. We wish that every decision we make is right. If people do not want their desires and wishes or selfishness to become dominant in the decisions they will make and consequently they or others get upset, they will want to make fair decisions.

In conclusion, whatever decision is made and whatever result is experienced, the option that this result is tolerable and just is only possible with the principle of fairness. This is because when a person makes a decision, they want it to be fair, and the result they will experience will be fair. This is because they acted fairly, knowing that they are not enslaved by their self-interests as they wanted their decision to be fair. Even if the result is not a desirable one, the person is at peace because they did their part. In other words, even if the result they desired did not occur, they are at peace because they did the "right" thing.

As we can understand from above, fairness forms the basis of humans' consciousness and belief systems and is the most fundamental starting point of the behaviours which operate in the infrastructure of people's life behaviours and decisions which are made in the name of justice, innocence, and paying the price or making someone else pay the price. In other words, fairness is at the top of the system of the universal laws that operate in us, and the other laws are associated with the operation here.

For this reason, we will address the operation of the system over both the dimension of humans' consciousness and the operating laws. Let's think about a social experiment that will help us better understand the sensitivity of this issue.

Imagine that you are the driver of a bus with 100 people on it, and there is one person on the road in front of you. You have the option to either sacrifice that one person and save the 100 people, or to save that one person and sacrifice the 100 people.

All of the subjects were of the opinion that 100 people would be more valuable and it would be more correct to sacrifice one person. When the same question was asked to the same subjects as what they would do if that one person was one of their relatives or loved ones, it was observed that the subjects' opinion changed, and they would sacrifice the 100 people for that one person.

Let's expand this question more and imagine that there are 100 vicious killers on the bus and the person on the road is our enemy, or assume that the people on the bus are scientists and that one person is someone we love. Let's look at people's answers and opinions and try to understand why the thing that affects our decision and opinion here is variable.

Similarly, let's prepare a population of 100 subjects and give a total of 100 sacs containing an equal number of, e.g., a hundred each, invaluable jewels to each subject. Let's tell the subjects that the jewels are randomly put into the sacs, that we do not know how many jewels there are in the sacs, and that their statements are essential, and ask them to say how many jewels there are in their sacs.

How many subjects do you think will say there are 100 jewels in their sacs? We guess that almost all of the subjects will say the number of jewels in their sacs to be lower than 100 and try to keep some of the jewels for themselves.

As can be seen in both experiments, we know that even though people think, say, or believe that they are being sincere, honest, or objective in the issues of sincerity, fairness, and justice, the truth is not, or cannot be, this way.

This is because we know the operating system and how this system operates or will operate. Here, the system is the active-passive system. This system determines people's momentary behaviour models. We represent the matter structure of the universe with the fact that our body (tangible existence) belongs to this universe and with our bodily existence. As a result of the existence of our body, our consciousness, which is connected to this bodily existence, is our active structure consciousness. In other words, this consciousness is our consciousness that is under the control of the emotional and receptor stimuli connected to our body. In this sense, it is an active structure that is connected to the energy system and operation of the universe. In other words, our structure that will sacrifice 100 people if the person on the road is someone we love while we are driving that bus with 100 people, is our active consciousness.

Our active consciousness is our side that will make a choice and bear whatever its consequences are, and that will make the same choice over and over again. This is because the control is in our matter structure and is based on the fact that we will always feel the same, and in the end, we will not be able to help protecting that one person every time due to what we call the instinct of protecting the person we love. In other words, the active hardware is our consciousness controlling us. Our active consciousness works focusing on the cause-and-effect relationship, and is our rational structure that will not say "No, I am not hungry!" when we are hungry or "No, it is not good, it is bad!" when a situation is good.

Our passive consciousness is our structure that we mistakenly considered if it does not belong to our body and thinks independently of our body (the structure outside of the receptor stimuli). In other words, it is our structure that we can deny as if it does not hurt even when a needle pricks our hand, or we try to hide as if we are not affected at all although an incident bothers us; in other words, where we try to hide our own reality and our real structure for any reason.

As in the above example of the bus, if we are active, in other words, if our emotional hardware consciousness is on, we can make different decisions; and if we are passive, we can again make different decisions.

If we do not know the people on the bus and that one person on the road, we can look at the event without passive consciousness and weigh the passive values such as justice and fairness. When we become a part of the event, then our active structure inevitably steps in and may lead us to different results. This structure is our structure which shows that our active consciousness is dominant and does what is necessary, taking the risk of having to pay the price when necessary. This structure is one that we cannot deny even though it does not make rational decisions according to social values. This is because the active form always comes first and is the determinant in the active-passive option. What we try to do in life is to try to write the passive values of justice, fairness and morals into our active hardware and to internalise them. This is because we want our decisions and choices to be fair. The core meaning of fairness is not the definition of events according to ourselves or someone else but the definition of events according to their own reality.

In other words, fairness is not the fact that what you or I say is true, but the fact that both of us accept and consent to what is the reality of that thing. This situation of everyone consenting is the decision or values that represent the common-mind and collective conscience. If we act upon our examples, there is also a possibility that in the future, we fall out and become enemies with that person we love and for whom we sacrificed 100 people. One of those 100 people may be a person who will intend to kill us, or a murderer that will kill 100 people intentionally.

As we cannot know which is going to happen, it means we actually do not know what fairness really is, either. Thus, this also means we cannot make a judgement about fairness. However, the fact that we cannot know what fairness is does not mean fairness will drive us to indecision when we exhibit a behaviour or make decisions. On the contrary, fairness will restrict us from acting arbitrarily and calibrate us when we make decisions. In addition, it will ensure that we take the possibility of making mistakes into consideration and prevent us from mistakenly thinking that "**this is absolutely true**".

Even if we, all the people living on Earth, come together and try to reach a consensus about what fairness is and reach a consensus, we cannot say that the thing upon which we reach a consensus is the measure of the fairness of that event. What we do will be the thing we want to happen or deem appropriate.

What is called fairness may be a different concept and we all may be mistaken for reasons we cannot know. For this reason, we should look to events on the basis of science and should not approach anything as absolute.

Let's give another example of why we cannot know what fairness is. Imagine that we are three people, and we have one loaf of bread in our hands. Fairness is to divide the bread into three, and when another person comes while we are dividing the bread into three, we have to divide it into a fourth. Imagine that a cat comes near us just while we are dividing the bread into four. The cat also has a share of the bread, and we must reserve a share for it, too. Apart from the shares to be reserved, there is also an issue of who is hungrier and needs the bread more, and we cannot know every possibility. We try to ensure fairness and justice over the measurements we know. If you attempt to determine fairness at your will, then you already do not have to give any shares to anyone anyway, and you can eat that loaf of bread as you want. However, when fairness steps in, you see that everyone and everything has a right to the bread. This is because if something is a right for you, then it is also a right for others. Rates may change, but right is right, and we cannot know the rate of the right holders or how many there are, and what happened or will happen. Therefore, we will never know the measure of fairness. For us, the measure of fairness will be what the common-mind and collective conscience reach a consensus upon. However, we all will also know and keep in mind that this measure of fairness is not absolute and there may be exceptions. Knowing the principle and presumption of fairness is the first step of being an "upright" person. Just like the first grade in primary school, it is the first stage of being human and a structure that we will be together throughout our lives. The more information we have about the fairness of an event, the more virtuous we will become in proportion to our knowledge. In other words, we can think that if we know 5 criteria for fairness regarding an event, we are a person of 5 points; and if we know 10 criteria, we are a person of 10 points. However, apart from knowing, we cannot neglect doing and carrying out what is known. If we do not do what is necessary although we know, this is already irresponsibility. Knowing and doing are equally weighted and co-ordinately operating systems.

There is another "self" in every person and every person knows that it exists. This "self," where the event is analysed together, and a fight is had, or a consensus is reached over the reason why it is done when a person makes a mistake or does an injustice, or when someone else acts in this way toward them, is a structure called the voice of the Creator, or the voice of conscience.

This voice is our connection with the creator's conscience and is our passive consciousness. This voice is the voice that is not shaped according to our bodily call but tells what should happen. In other words, the voice that tells us to eat when we feel hungry is our **active** consciousness that belongs to our bodies. Our consciousness regarding which food will be appropriate and what the option will be when we feel hungry is our **passive** consciousness. This choice is our consciousness that makes comparison, interpretation, and questioning. As long as we live, our bodily consciousness is **active**; our consciousness regarding the existence of our dreams, wishes, and choices is the **passive** consciousness. Our passive consciousness is how we will carry out events, but actually, we cannot be indifferent to our active consciousness. In other words, our consciousness that says that we should appease our hunger is our active consciousness that we cannot be indifferent to in any case.

Nevertheless, the issue of how we will appease our hunger is passive and it comes after the active one and can be postponed. Our passive consciousness is our guide consciousness regarding doing what is right. We are inspired by these; in other words, we copy them. However, the consciousness that carries out the event is our bodily consciousness. This is our consciousness that we call "me" and define as ourselves; in other words, the active structure is our consciousness.

Our passive consciousness, which is the creator consciousness in us, tells us:

> **"Without me, you would not exist, nor would the universe."**
> **"You see these as I exist, and you think you exist."**
> **"If I did not exist, nothing would exist, and thus, I am the one that created and brought into existence everything."**

Against this, our bodily consciousness says:

> **"If I did not exist as the body and the organ called brain, you would not exist anyway. Thus, actually, you owe your existence to me."**

These two structures are the symmetry of each other at the same time. Existing and operating at the same time constitutes the essence of the activeness-passiveness and is also a necessity. You cannot separate any of them from each other or take and defend them individually as determinant elements.

Here, in the operating system, our active structure is our bodily consciousness as we exist in the universe, and we are in the universe with a matter structure. Our passive consciousness is our connection with the consciousness in the universe that created the universe.

Thanks to the combination of these two consciousnesses, we are thinking (comprehending) creatures, and an increase in this combination means our bodily consciousness better understands and comprehends the creator consciousness.

When we look at the structure of the universal laws operating in humans, we can comprehend and understand that the structure which should exist in humans predicts that humans are equal and free individuals and love is dominant. The way to ensure this should be completely rational and fair practices, and as a reference, observation of fairness for everyone. People have two extreme behaviours (due to the law of symmetry). One of them is pain and the other is happiness and peace. If the aim is to make a person suffer, as a necessity, they will also want to hurt you because they will want you to experience the pain they experience. This is because the law of action and reaction will step in here, and that person will try to explain to you what they feel by making you experience what you have made them experience and by hurting you.

This mutual hurting does not have an end, and this process continues until one destroys the other. This is a way that will not bring happiness and peace anyway, because neither the one who gets hurt, nor the one who hurts, can be pleased. This is because the fact that a person is happy when they get hurt is against the law of the instrument and the one who hurts will experience a disturbance of conscience and empathy (symmetry). In this case, there will be no chance to be happy and in peace for either party (situations excluding pathological cases). This situation is a valid system that operates for every contrary situation like wealth and poverty, or good and bad, in addition to the situations such as ego contests and jealousy.

Humans' other choice of behaviour is based on happiness and peace. Here, the contest is about "I love you more" or "I am more self-sacrificing for you than you are for me." However, there is a secret, unnoticed ego operation here. Even though the statement is about love, there is still an effort to establish superiority and create difference. Therefore, there is a fear and uneasiness of being subordinate to the other party and, in fact, there is not proper happiness and peace. For this contest not to begin, it is necessary that people are **equal and equivalent**. Equal and equivalent individuals live their love as they wish (naturally), not over being less or more. If this makes both parties happy, what is done is not perceived as an element of contest.

People are happy and feel free because they live as they wish and are reciprocated. This is the only way to feel free (of course, the fact that freedom also involves respect, kindness and compassion should not be forgotten).

Thus, we can say that the way to live humanely is equity, freedom, and love. This also shows that fairness is established, and you cannot ensure fairness without these main components, anyway. In other words, actually, when you look at the operation of the system, you can see that for something to exist, it is required that the factors creating it also exist. If we want peace and brotherhood, we must understand and see that fairness, justice, equity, freedom and love are the principles and operations that work connected to each other.

If we build these principles and operations, the necessities that we know the entirety of humanity is a family and that the problems such as exploitation, cruelty, unfair management, unfair judgement order and inequality in income distribution are inevitably linked. In this entire operation, we can predict that humanity will eventually see the truth and manage to act humanely, or they have to manage this.

Let's try to follow the effects of fairness in our current lives in the cause-effect operation by trying to understand fairness over the energy system. We should understand fairness as the place that represents the point where it is the exact symmetry or point of the law of symmetry; in other words, the exact point of separation between good and bad, or the point where the scale pans are exactly equal, or the point where active and passive forms are separated from each other. We can look at its operation in human relationships through an example. For example, you are so sure of the fact that your mother is old-fashioned, and she does not, or cannot, understand you about an issue that you think your mother definitely cannot see a detail you see. This is because you are convinced that you have thought everything that can be thought about that issue, and your mother cannot think of something different from what you have thought, and thus, you also think for her and determine that it is impossible for her to understand you. You claim that your mother does not understand you as you are sure of yourself, and you try to explain yourself to her. You are so sure of your righteousness that you make an effort to explain the situation to her at the cost of hurting her. Although your aim is not to hurt your mother, you insist because you think your mother should understand some things now. Finally, you achieve your goal and make your mother give in. Your mother withdraws telling you to do whatever you want. Just when you think you did something good and enabled your mother to see some things from your perspective, you realise that what you have defended also has a different aspect. While you found yourself right until a little while ago, you then face the fact that the situation has suddenly changed, and you are wrong. You realise that you did injustice while you thought you were right and that your mother was subjected to injustice although she was right.

The situation has turned into the opposite of your initial intention. Your mother was aggrieved; however, you were actually aggrieved, too. This is because you became aggrieved as a cause that you did not know emerged and you could not see it before. This time, you will start trying to make your mother forgive you in order to compensate for this aggrievement. If your mother does not forgive you, then you will think about why your mother acts unconsciously and does not forgive you, presuming that you would make a mistake.

This fluctuation stems from the result that you do not, or cannot, know the fairness point of balance of the issue that you claimed. Although fairness has an infinite number of possibilities and you think you know all of them, you should comprehend that there can be a possibility of +1 that you cannot know – thus, you cannot say "**Even God would decide this.**" What is experienced here is your or your mother's effort to balance the energy system or meet at the centre of symmetry and the effort for the active-passive structure to meet at the same point.

As another example, imagine that a man loves a woman. The man does not share his feelings clearly and interprets her intimacy or interest toward him as if she loves him in his mind. As he believes this, he proposes to her in a crowded place to both honour his loved one and show the courage he took from his love. However, she regards his proposal and his love for her as crossing the line.

In another example, a gardener working in a farm interprets the humane behaviour of the daughter in the house as if she is interested in him and proposes to her. Similarly, the daughter of the farmer perceives this proposal as crossing the line.

Here, what men think and take as an argument is their point of view that everyone is human and thus the active thing is humans themselves and their love and that status, money and other things are passive. However, in the case where the argument women consider active is an expectation of status, money, etc., except for the other's love and humanity, a conflict of active and passive is experienced between the parties.

Here, the conclusions are that active and passive structures are not clearly specified, not everyone acts with their activeness, and these factors are incompatible. Another conclusion is the fact that giving up on passiveness is easier, but you cannot give up on passiveness. In any case, what determines the faith or process of the event is not the passive structure but the active structure (the passive structure can never be the active structure unless it is internalised).

What determines people's activeness-passiveness here is the learned values. Despite the truth that everyone is human in essence, all other structures such as status, money, position, etc., are passive. What we call preference consists of choices and people have learned this passiveness due to right or wrong reasons. This learning is based on basic instincts in primitive men, such as nutrition, reproduction, and shelter. Fundamentally, fairness is a passive structure, but we can never give up on it because that is what makes us human.

We try to turn our active structure into this passive structure; in other words, we internalise it. People will prevent all misunderstandings or injustices if they observe the principle of fairness. As long as this is followed, no problems will be experienced.

The main goal of being human is to move humans' own activeness to the nice passive structures within the measures of fairness, integrating with it, and internalising those nice passive structures. In other words, it is the fact that humans internalise nice passive structures and make them their own activeness. To state it differently, it is the fact that humans adopt and internalise common-mind principles and values.

What we call internalisation is actually a kind of software. It is the uploading of the passive fairness values onto our active hardware. In other words, it is the uploading of the software in our active hardware onto the hardware, and when this upload is done, people understand the responsibility of being "human". To state it differently, it is the inspection and synchronisation of our both active and passive structures.

When we look at the events from the perspective of fairness, is being a gazelle or a lion a crime in the world we live in? What we consider the most humanistic is if lions did not feed on gazelles. However, in this case, we must find a solution for how the lion will feed. This requires us to find a solution for the food chain. When we adapt this to the entire system operating in the universe, we see that there is an energy transfer on nutrition. In other words, strong current manages the weak current, or the one with high gravitation draws the one with low gravitation. Instead of making the good-bad separation of this transfer, we must eliminate the need for energy transfer. This phenomenon of needing is a part of the operating system that we cannot change. What is called fairness is the conditions that determine the choices for balancing this. So, how is the good-bad, crime-punishment operation created in our consciousness structure during this energy transfer?

The infrastructure of crime is based on the principle of energy necessity. For us to judge a lion for eating a gazelle, we must know the fundamental dynamics of this, or the dynamics of a murderer to commit a murder, or the dynamics of defending the righteousness of our wish to stop the lion when we understand that the lion will kill a gazelle. The reasons that create the results may be of an infinite number; however, the action that will be the determining factor is single and is what commits the crime.

If the event occurred as a result of an accident without a reason, only then can innocence be mentioned. Other than that, fairness should be sought even if there is only one reason, and if fairness is already sought, it means justice has become unbalanced (the balance of energy).

The desired punishment is the sanction regarding the establishment of this balance. First, if there is a crime, it is necessary that the criminal bear the punishment to be imposed. The fact that this punishment is fair is the most fundamental operation that the parties seek. However, none of us can know what fairness is, and no one can say, "Even God gives this punishment."

What we will consider as fairness here is the common mind and collective conscience. The basis of justice is this conscientious judgement. Absolute fairness is not in question. Based on the fundamental principle that "law does not know the one who does not know, or one who impairs the system bears its consequence," if there is a crime, aggrievement will exist in any case, and the parties will not be satisfied.

The criterion of our fairness closest to real fairness is the criterion that we can make the same decision "even if it is a decision that will cause our death". In the end, crime is a result, and results are our concern. The intention of the crime is the criminal's concern. Our primary goal and responsibility should be that crime does not occur, and for this, everyone should have responsibility.

6

PRINCIPLE OF SINCERITY

Sincerity is an indispensable and basic principle that makes a person an "upright" human. There is no need for another definition to explain the importance of sincerity. Everybody who can understand this already knows this fact.

If you really understand yourself, you question your sincerity. Be sincere even while questioning your sincerity. If you can achieve sincerity, then you will be the person that you should be.

The beginning of sincerity is based on the operation of the management of our basic instincts. If our defence mechanism does not work based on specific principles, it works based on the principle of protection of the person according to their own natural protection. This is a system that will work irrespective of the concepts of right-wrong or good-bad.

The concepts of right-wrong are the values which we upload to our hardware as software. In other words, they are universal and scientific principles and acceptances. If we do not have principal rights, our defence mechanisms make decisions in line with our feeling good irrespective of looking after others' rights. Defence mechanisms work focusing on trust and risks since their function is based on the protection foundation, and take your interests as a matter of priority in any case.

Even when you do wrong, defence mechanisms do not question it if you get an interest from this wrong thing. However, if you are determined to do the right thing, your defence mechanism will only then make the right and wrong judgements. If you wish, and are determined to do the right thing in any case, and avoid doing the wrong for your own interests, your defence mechanisms will work depending on your principles and determination.

For this reason, it is a must for us to have principles to be a good person. Otherwise, we can make very changeable and inconsistent decisions, and as a result, we can both aggrieve other people or be aggrieved.

The energy part of this operation, in other words, hardware infrastructure, is associated with neurology and biochemistry. We will examine the basic principles of consciousness reflecting on our senses.

The consciousness infrastructure of the sincerity operation is a system that is based on unknowability and acceptance. In other words, it is being yourself and saying what you think as well as your choice to act based on the other party making assumptions in line with the expectations of others. Of course, every person has their own acceptances and these do not change easily from event to event. However, if you use acceptances to persuade the other party instead of your own acceptances according to the other party, it means you cannot be sincere. This is because this is your selection of the references of the other party instead of your own references so as not to get reaction, because you do not rely on your acceptances and principles. This results in distrust in people regarding how to behave and in which condition. People close their minds to you and become defensive. If you suppose that insincerity is not noticed, and you will seek denial even if it is noticed, you will be wrong. This is because just at this point, sincerity is being honest to yourself, being sure that the insincerity is understood, and not condescending to insincerity. If you suppose that it cannot be understood, you should know that you deceive yourself. This is because if a person is doing wrong, it is not because they do not know, as they mostly do it on purpose. This is just what should be noticed. If a person is doing wrong, they are doing so by relying on themselves and without feeling responsible – with the understanding of "who will prevent this?" not, "according to what?" or "according to whom?" it is wrong. Yes, maybe nobody can persuade that person about this wrong deed. This is because denialism is already insincere and you cannot prove the denial. However, the question that should be responded to is whether or not they would accept a reason for the justification of this wrongdoing when that wrongdoing is done to themselves rather than another person.

If this person does not accept this wrongdoing or tolerates it in any way, then they cannot expect others to accept or tolerate it. You should be sure that if something seems wrong to you, it will seem wrong to every person on Earth because all of us have the same references and principles.

Every person that lives and breathes on Earth cannot present a single justifiable reason that something that is wrong, according to these principles, will be right. This is because all of us know that, in fact, it is, and should be so. If someone is trying to make an excuse, in fact, we all already know that this person is not sincere. The person who makes the excuse already knows that this is an excuse and that it is not correct.

As can be seen, people's acceptances carry on the assumption that "others cannot know" what they know is actually choosing the method of denialism and insincerity instead of reality. This is because every person on Earth knows that it is true although they do not want to believe it.

Now that we all know this, then we should choose the behaviour that suits us, get rid of the insincerity of deceiving ourselves and not bother with this. What we should understand and face is that such manoeuvres erode our prestige and people lose their trust in us. Therefore, I hope all humanity will immediately comprehend and understand that there is no other option than sincerity.

In the environments you are familiar with or know, the system that works first in you operates based on the **threat-trust** basis. It starts first with the perception that everything is a threat to prevent the risk. The environment and the people are tested and this continues until an element of trust is formed. In other words, the scales of the balance are initially filled with the elements of threat. As you become familiar with the environment or people, we remove the threatening elements and balance the trust element on this scale.

Well, how can we understand whether a person we do not know at all is a threat to us or not? If we take it reversely, the people we deal with will regard us as threats since they do not know us.

Because the law of symmetry will work here, we should never forget that every event has two elements in any case (good-bad, sincere-crooked, honest-hypocritical, etc.) Therefore, we can exhibit two attitudes towards the people who do not know us. The first is being sincere and acting as we are. The second is behaving universally and specifying the priority according to the behaviour of the other party. You should not forget that the other party will do the same at the same time while we are doing this. If the other party feigns so as not to make us uneasy, although they are hypocritical, it will take us time to understand this. We will have to feign to understand the other party; as the phrase goes, "two acrobats cannot dance on the same rope".

No matter, good or bad, if we take the other party as a basis for our behaviour or if we have the expectation that "first the other party shows their true colour", we will do wrong and have problems in any case. This is because we will not be able to know the intention of every person, and we will not be able to have the chance to know them. We are aggrieved on the road we take to protect ourselves in any case, get tired, in any case and get personally hurt. Now, for this reason, we should be ourselves and behave like ourselves in any case.

If we are really a good person, the other party will soon understand that we are ourselves and are not acting. If we are not a good person, we will be deciphered soon enough, and we provide people with the opportunity to make us pay the price as we cheat them without being satisfied with our wrongdoing. Therefore, we will be at risk of suffering twice as much.

If you think that "we behave like ourselves, but people do not honour our real personality", you will be wrong. This is because instead of acting like somebody else, and being deciphered in the end, be yourself in any case, so those who love and honour you honour "your own state".

If people do not honour you although you are really a good person, it means they do not deserve you anyway. If you say, "I behave like myself, and everybody may honour me," although you are not a proper person, think of the law of symmetry and ask, "would you honour yourself if you were in the other party's shoes?"

If you do not honour yourself, be sure that others will also not honour you. Of course, today if you have money and power, many people seem as if they honour you, but you will know that this is a fake honour. Sincerity is the distinction between remaining honest or not, just in the determination stage of a person's action or statement. In other words, it is like a "last exit before the bridge" on a highway.

Human hardware is a system that is based on the principle of people's making a preference by themselves between the understanding of,

> "**I am a human, and I cannot know and do everything. I do or say what I find right. However, what I find right can also be wrong, and I can be wrong, so I can make mistakes,**"

and

> "**Although I do not know everything, I say what I find to be right. If a problem is experienced, I pretend I didn't mean it. I say, I did not mean that",**

and that functions on this basis. In other words, it is a preference between being sincere and handling the situation or the choice between taking and not taking responsibility. Being the addressees of the issue, we actually understand that this is like this but cannot be sure which choice is made. To test why the relevant expression is made, we seem to accept the principle "statement is essential," but we wait without making a judgement until we become sure. If there is no responsibility for sincerity, it means the essence of sincerity is not achieved. In other words, if people do not feel responsible for what they do or say, they cannot be expected to be sincere as well. Therefore, sincerity and responsibility cannot be separated from each other. The essence of sincerity and responsibility is still fairness as well.

People's expectations of you may be different from what you think. Real sincerity is behaving in accordance with **what fairness requires** and regarding fairness rather than behaving in a way the other party expects from you or in a way that you find right.

Sincerity is being able to take responsibility and stand behind what you say if you are wrong. Saying the thing that you cannot stand behind is irresponsible and also insincere. If you understand that you are wrong although you say you really believe, it is still your responsibility to correct yourself and apologise.

So it means that being sincere includes both responsibility and determination. If you become more like yourself, everybody will put you in the place where they intend to put you, but nobody will turn back and tell you, "You cheated me."

Doing this, you will find the freedom of being human. You will neither get tired nor cause suffering in someone to be a person that people approve of. On the contrary, you will set an example for people who are thirsty for sincerity.

You will have lived this life, not according to the rights of other people, but to your own rights (universal rights). If you are really a good person, you will be held in high regard by those who deserve and love you, though not others.

And you know that people around you stand by you because they really love you and consider you valuable. I suppose you, as well, are aware of how precious that is today.

The tragicomic aspect of this is everybody plays ostrich and thinks that the other party does not understand this. However, everybody is aware of the situation, and if they happen to say directly to the relevant person that "Your intention is this," they know that this person will deny it. They even brazen the matter out and are ready to scold the other party saying, "Hey, how do you think about me like this?" To top it all off, they do not confine themselves and make a fool of you, saying, "What did I do to make you think this about me, so you are unfair to me?" But guys, if you feel this way about the other party, you are possibly not wrong in your feelings. This is because if it is not so, you already cannot feel that it is like this. This is because if the hardware in yourself perceives this, it is almost true.

When we feel that the other party is not sincere, we all experience the indecision that, **"maybe, I am wrong in my feeling"**, but trust in the system that operates in yourself. This is because even if you are not aware, if your inner radar has caught on to this, it should absolutely have a foundation.

People may not suppose that the other party cannot understand or feel what they think about inside. This is definitely not true, and the hardware inside you is certainly aware of the situation. Moreover, even if it is true, if you feel something about someone, it is at least certain that there is an insincerity. If someone makes it feel, this person should know that they did not behave adequately sincerely, and you realise this.

This is not an intention reading and this case is the operation of hardware in you. Know this fact and behave accordingly; neither cheat yourself nor make a fool of the other party. First, be "human" and be yourself. Believe that you will be very happy and free.

Another operation of sincerity is about our life experiences. Imagine that you made a mistake in the past. You made a mistake and regret it, realising that what you did was wrong. When you see the issue from your perspective, you think, "everybody can make mistakes, therefore, I made a mistake, and it should be forgiven". However, when you put yourself in the shoes of the other party, mistakes have been made to you, and your confidence is broken. On the one hand, it is thought that mistakes are acceptable and they should be forgiven. If a person does not forgive the mistake, there should be an accusation against the other party as to why they do not forgive the mistake. On the other hand, the accusation of aggrievement and cheating the other party is in question because of not being sincere. In fact, people become both aggrieved, and they aggrieve others in the actions they do without feeling responsible. People who are aggrieved by someone lose the feeling of trust. In such a case, people have to play it safe towards everybody to protect themselves and prejudices occur. Moreover, these cases of aggrievement can be used as an excuse, justification and opportunity for evil-minded people's own irresponsibility.

As can be seen, being sincere is necessary in any case so as not to experience such breaking. The way of being sincere is possible by hoping to be fair in all cases.

This is because the principle of fairness will prevent all excuses and breakups.

Sincerity has also a courage dimension. "Although they are sincere in their intentions, they cannot behave sincerely because of their lack of courage." Indeed, this case is also a fact of a person escaping from coming face to face with themselves.

Some people may sincerely believe that they know what is correct about an issue. However, these people have no courage to do what they know. These people may encourage others to make them do what they know and have the intention to realise this for themselves (even if the person is not aware of this, this is a system that operates in their hardware).

This case is actually lacking in courage, is irresponsible and insincere. While the person attributes this only to their lack of courage, they actually avoid facing themselves. When the results of a case that occurs are correct, they will take credit for themselves, saying, "I encouraged it." If this case ends with a wrong result, they will have the opportunity to test what they have defended to others since they will not have to pay for wrongdoing.

As can be seen, not sincerity, but slyness is in question in all of these cases. In other words, these are the efforts for managing the situation without taking risks and also trying to hide that they are being insincere (people may be doing this without even being aware of it).

In fact, people think they are not noticed while doing this, but they are wrong. If you can think like this and make a plan, others can understand whether you have done this or not. When you are told that this is your intention, you think that you have the chance to deny and refute, but you are still wrong. Because people cannot prove this, they act as if they believe in you, but they do not, and know that you are insincere. **In other words, what is important is not people's saying whether you are sincere or not, but their believing whether you are sincere or not.** As can be easily understood, there is no need for such manoeuvres. Because there is neither the deceived person nor the deceiving person in the essence of the matter, and everybody is aware of the case of your insincerity. Again, there is need for the principle of justice so as not to need all of these manoeuvres.

If steps are taken paying regards to fairness in every desired or done event, the results will inevitably be as they are required to be. Otherwise, aggrievement and negativity will be experienced. Even if you set forth with the principle of fairness and a negative result is achieved, it is easy to compensate for it. This is because there is no evil intention – it is easy to forgive and ask for forgiveness.

In all these thought fluctuations, we should comprehend that our being fair and sincere is the only inevitable option.

THE OPERATION OF EGO IN HUMANS

(The operation of the principle of symmetry balance in humans)

The origin of the operation called ego or selfness is related to comprehending the principle of symmetry balance. The origin of this operation is the failure to comprehend the principles of the symmetry separation like good-bad or "I"-"you" in our comprehension. Failure to know that the system will not operate smoothly without the balance principles in question is the origin of selfness. The principle of fairness determines and operates the separation point in humans called I-you or the other (consciousness). A person who acts with "selfness" disregards the balance in the separation of I-you and is in false safety, and wrong that they will form and operate this balance according to themselves. In this case, the mistake of the determination of fairness according to their own perspective or interest is in question. This is a kind of mistake where a person determines justice and fairness according to the balance they have formed and has convinced themselves that this is not a problem. However, the laws and principles of the universe are available just for these. This is because you cannot establish and operate these balances according to yourself. The operation will eventually collapse, the system will make you pay, and it will come into balance. If a person does not comprehend this balance and disregards the other side of the symmetry, in other words, other people and attempts to operate the system according to the rules established by themselves, this case psychologically emerges as negative situations such as selfishness, arrogance, ambition, unlimitedness, lies, betrayals, slander, insincerity and hypocrisy.

Instead of the fairness principles, which are the system's own control mechanisms, the defence mechanism, as they operate according to the selfness of the person, has to be an instrument to these problems to protect the person. To avoid all of them from occurring, the system should comprehend its own principles and interiorize them. These are the principles of fairness, sincerity, and responsibility. We consider all these principles as ego and selfness of humans.

Selfness: It is a state of loneliness that does not comply with the rules, establishes its own rules, and considers everything apart from itself as a threat against them. This is because selfness admires itself, and it is a state of obsession that considers itself superior to everybody and convinces itself that it is more special than everybody else. Selfness is a state of blindness that believes them to be smart, intelligent, and ahead of everybody else in terms of craftiness. It considers themselves a soft touch compared to themselves and who believes that everybody is cheatable compared to themselves. Selfness does not believe in principles and values because it does not comply with any rules and does not have respect for anything. This perception is a personality disorder that sees everybody as sacrificable and disposable for the sake of their own peace, comfort and interests because of not having respect for anything.

Let's examine the comparison between the selfless perception and the reference perception of the system with an example. For example, while a person is explaining an event, a person with a perception of selfness concludes that the faulty party is the other party, if the other party does not understand what is explained and does not find it necessary to question themselves. This is because this person becomes arrogant, thinking that they did what was necessary according to them, but the other party is faulty because they do not understand this. However, the reference perception of the system is the perception that "I cannot explain, so the other party does not explain". This is because nobody is obliged to know what you know, and you cannot think that these people are obliged to understand you. What you explain is valuable for yourself, so it is you who wants to explain it. If you attach importance to your explanation, you cannot disregard the fact that it is under your responsibility to explain this to the other party correctly. If what you explain is really unimportant, you will not mind whether the other party understands or not. In other words, if what you explain is unimportant, you will not question why the other party did not understand, and you will not have a perception of accusation because the other party did not understand.

This means selfness is the operation of considering everything important because it considers itself important, and underestimating and accusing the other party because it does not understand this. However, if you were using the principles of the system, you would not disregard the option that "the other party cannot understand you because you cannot explain it".

Again, if you were to use the principles of the system, you would put yourself into the other party's shoes with the belief that the other party is a match for you, feel the perception that "I wonder how I would prefer this to be explained to me if I were in their shoes?" and behave in a way in which you want them to understand you. This is because people behave toward you in a way you behave to them.

Therefore, the expression, "If you want to be loved, learn how to love, and if you want to be respected, learn how to respect", is not said for nothing. Thus, we should internalise the requirement to act without accusing people or regarding ourselves as superior to them in our behaviours towards others. How do you know that you are superior? If others consider you superior or you consider yourself superior, this does not mean that you are really superior. If you try to be worthy of this appreciation of people instead of thinking that you deserve people seeing you as superior, only then will you really be worthy of being superior. Otherwise, it is arrogance and selflessness. Superiority is possible only by **merit**, not by people's wishes.

If people with selfness are told the fact that they are as human as everybody, and everybody is like themselves, people whom they consider to have a soft touch will not bother with these problems because they do not actually have a soft touch but are virtuous, and in fact, none of this is necessary, and if these people comprehend this fact, then they will recover from this sickness of selfness and will become happy and peaceful.

I am sure that everybody has forgotten much of their memories from childhood. The memories which have remained in their memories are either bad or good things about their childhood. In fact, these memories are the first breakups in the emotions of humans. However, memories of your own childhood are the same as those who lived in the cave period. No matter where on Earth a person is born, they cannot know what kind of a place the world is where they have first opened their eyes; they get hungry, feel cold, fear, or get hurt. They cannot know whether only they, or everybody, experiences this, and whether everybody is like them or not; they try to understand and make sense of what they experienced. When someone hurts them, they are not aware of the reason for this. They cannot know whether what they believe is the return of their life or the result from another cause, and they try to learn this. A human being tries to comprehend whether the things they encounter in their life are caused by themselves, or are the responsibility of another party. When you are hurt for the first time, you cannot make sense of the reason why you are experiencing this. You suppose that everybody experiences what you do and gets hurt, and this continues until you comprehend the cause and effect relationship of what is experienced, and understand which one is your error and which one is the error of others. The process called education and learning includes different events in everybody's life, and many traumatic events are observed or experienced. Systems operating here are the mixed combination of the laws of cause and effect, active-passive form and symmetry.

The process of obscurity is experienced until you comprehend the reason for the occurrence of events. Everybody eventually analyses the dynamics of life in their own way, becoming aware of what they will do or not, and they participate among the players of the scene.

The basic acceptance and argument

The basic acceptance and argument of a human is approval, caring about, and loving the fact of a person being directly human in their pure and plain state, ignoring the physical appearance and wishes, social family status, or any other title of this human. In other words, it is based on being taken into consideration, approved, or cared about just because they are human. However, this person observes, and soon realises that there is discrimination between people, and they are separated with different expectations, statuses and titles. Evaluating a person in a different way than their friend although they do the same things, protecting their friend due to family status or for another reason, their being punished, or being questioned while ignoring what their friend did.

What people realise first in this example is the feeling of injustice. Humans face the fact that being an "upright" person is not adequate and other passive things are requested, or at least people do a separation with such an expectation. Here, this case brings about the opinion and belief that although people are equal as "humans", this equality is broken due to other intentions and reasons of humans, people take sides caring about one side more and prizing that side, they are subjected to injustice, they are not treated fairly, and justice is broken.

These breakups trigger defence mechanisms, and the operating principles in our hardware become involved. Eliminating the discomfort caused by this situation makes way for the person to seem and act differently than they actually are.

Humans try to find a method for coping with, and overcoming these.

They try to find the most viable way to cope with many attributes such as intelligence, hard work, being rich, poor, skilful and hundreds of others.

This operation of finding solutions is the first software practice you did to your hardware, and your hardware is now the behaviour model where you say which way you behave will be more proper behaviour.

Therefore, it is the conclusion of this software practice what type of a person the human will be.

In fact, we can run the hardware according to the new software by updating the software. In other words, we can fix ourselves and become a proper person.

The most valued method today is to be rich and famous. The second option that can be deemed as average is to choose a position that will be affected less by discrimination. This is the target of gaining status through good education and finding a good job to earn enough money so as not to need anybody.

This is today's most popular software and is the updated software practice until it evolves into another software practice.

Therefore, people of specific generations begin life with these software programs.

Under these circumstances and when a person selects these as the target for themselves, obstacles that will come their way also begin to deem wrongdoings reasonable. They do not abstain from sacrificing their humanistic values if they find it necessary to achieve the aim. This is because their humanity is not worthy; values that are worthy become more valuable to them, and all of these are breakups and erosions.

When the person attains their goal, they postpone their responsibilities and convince themselves that they will compensate for the wrongs they did. Because they believe they were aggrieved, they now have an excuse for everything, and therefore believe they are right while doing all of these.

We should incontrovertible accept that all these are wrong operations. This is because these are all the results of the wrong choices we made at the beginning. Nobody has the right and competence to say, "I did and it happened." This is because we are all actually the same and nobody can have superiority over another. For example, what is the crime of a person who was born disabled? We could be in their shoes and have experienced what they experienced. This is because being born disabled is not our own choice that makes us superior. It is adequate for you to become yourself, no matter what you will be.

If you put up an ego fight with someone, you will get hurt in any case and become eroded.

If someone attempts to behave egotistically to you, remember the law of symmetry, put yourself in their shoes and think whether it is worth it or not. Suppose that someone behaved egotistically to you, and you crushed them with your own ego. This person actually behaved egoistically because they suffered agony and they could not have tolerance, and you caused them to suffer agony twice more by crushing them. Maybe you destroy them in a way by giving them no leg to stand on to hold on in life. Let them become happy behaving egotistically and feeling superior to you, and do not bother to oppress them. Let them become happy thinking that they oppressed you because they have done because they needed it. If you know and are sure of yourself, no ego can oppress you because you are what you are. Being human and remaining as a human is in a place where no ego can compete, and the value of that cannot be made a matter of debate.

When we look at the other side of the coin, I seem to hear the question, "Aye, what then? Should we say hardly anything for people whose ego has gone through the roof?" Of course, I do not say let's give them a medal for what they have done. Let's warn them and enable them to see themselves, but compete with our egos like them and avoid being suspicious of our humanity. This is because otherwise, there will be no difference between us and them, and we become one of them.

We already know that the operation of defence mechanisms in our brain that forms the human consciousness is very fast. Our mechanism is in partial control while we are doing an act or making an expression. In other words, we know our own principles, and our hardware strives to work in accordance with these principles. However, we cannot directly understand, be sure of, or comprehend what the intention of others in their actions and statements toward us is. Because the working principle of our own hardware is programmed according to the law of action and reaction in others' actions and statements towards us; your hardware can sometimes operate without giving us a chance to check and can give reactions that we do not want.

Once you realize this, you may be too late. This can be observed more frequently in cases about prejudice and being conditioned. This is because your hardware is already prejudiced; it can behave as a reflex and misguide you. This is like passing through a forest with an express train and you cannot see the details or entirety of the landscape. You have to slow down and be aware of the landscape you are passing through to see the details. For example, people can very easily pass judgement without thinking or evaluating. Your hardware can have justified reasons, but you always have a margin of error. The justification of the system working in your hardware is mostly a person reaching the point of "**Who, other than me, can put up with what I suffer from, so I endure and bear it,**" being convinced of and passing judgement that no reference remained to endure the event. Therefore, it is easy to pass judgement (this is because the person wants to quickly discharge the energy on the system). What is actually difficult is to understand how we easily reached this judgement. In other words, it is the landscape you will see when you slow down the train. For example, someone's passing judgement on you with prejudice disturbs you. The perception and reflex that "**Who the hell are they to pass a judgement so quickly without knowing who I am?**" occurs to you. In fact, what you and the other party did is the same thing, and it is judging. Maybe because your justification seems reasonable to you, you can consider yourself right, but what has been done in the essence of the matter is the same.

When we slow down the train, in other words, when we have a chance to think a little before passing judgement, and when we try to understand why we passed this judgement or whether the judgement from the other party about us is right or not, we see the truth. In other words, it becomes apparent whether the other party, or we, are right.

Here, when we slow down to understand this event, in other words, when we give ourselves an opportunity to think about it, what we are actually trying to do, and what we find is the principle of **fairness**. Because what is tried to be understood is actually the questioning whether the justification is reasonable or not. In short, "was the justification passed fair or was it a mistake?"

There is always a case of looking for a crime and passing justification when a crime is found in the operational infrastructure of prejudice. Looking for a crime in someone is a person's being obstinate with, and placing a bet on themselves. Looking for a crime is always looking for fault in people believing that everybody has or will have a fault. It is feeling justified, being relieved, and satisfied when you find fault with the verification that "Look, I already knew that there would be a fault."

In fact, looking for a crime and fault is a person's failure to comprehend that they have faults in the essence of the matter. This is because trying to look for faults, although there is no fault, is a prejudice and an obsession. Because the seeking is always in line with finding a fault, all other structures and values will be missed and skipped. This case is actually the situation of a train quickly passing through the forest and hundreds of landscapes missed. Therefore, take it easy and do not look for faults (this is because there is no perfect person). If the other party has a fault, this person will let on themselves anyway, even if you are not looking for it.

You are not obliged to know and learn everything. It is enough for you to know what you require. Your knowing the fault and private doings of someone or your knowing the information, which is the sensitivity of that person, does not make you a wise person. On the contrary, it makes you a nosey and impertinent person. Just as you are ashamed when you make a mistake, are embarrassed and wish it had never happened, others will have the same sensitivity, and your wishing to learn this is not a skill but an improper curiosity.

No matter what you are trying to do, you cannot escape from the fact that we are human in the end. Now that you are human, know everybody is like yourself and behave in that way. Do not do anything to the other party that you do not want to be done to you. **This is because a person does not have the right to consider themselves as having the right for a behaviour they do not consider themselves to deserve.**

These values and principles are the values that are necessary for a person to be an "upright" human, and they must exist. For example, we all deem our mothers holy and that they are so valuable we cannot even define them with a value. This is because they are the people who brought us into the world and gave us life and spirit. By which value can you assess your mother in the universe, or let others assess?

Well, when you ask, "What makes my mother so precious?" you will see that there are basic values in its foundation such as compassion, love, understanding, and tolerance, which should exist in its foundation. Now that they are priceless values, then try to embrace them. Just as these values are the values you need, do not forget that everybody is like you. No matter how much you behave capriciously and make mischief, or behave intentionally, or unintentionally presumptuously and unfairly, your mother cannot hurt you. You circle around and see your error and resort to their compassion.

You see your mother is valuable because of harbouring these values. This is because no matter what you do, your mother has not given up her upright character and her motherhood, and she is priceless as she has remained upright in all circumstances. Your mother is a human too, and maybe she suffered from injustice many times more than you. Yet, she does not hesitate to give all that she can and she tries to solve your pain by hiding her sorrow.

If a person does not know the value and meaning of these, it means they are inhuman. This is because a person should have these values first to be able to criticise or judge something. Therefore, we should inevitably have humanitarian values because this case is actually the result of our not having the right to choose, and if we are human, we should have these values.

It's not as if thousands of people like you haven't come and gone before you, and all of them disappeared as if they had never lived. Moreover, these people have come and gone without knowing what love, value and humanity are. Tears of today are the work of irresponsibility, lovelessness and selfishness of the past. If we do not want the future to be like this, we should correct something, starting today.

Sincerity, ego, and selfishness are competing head to head. Whenever you select ego and selfishness, it means one more tear will drop. As a result of this operation, you will eventually shed this tear. Even though we cannot manage to be sincere, we at least should not honour ego.

In the level of consciousness, there are choices that we all live and do not take into consideration or attach importance to. We cannot be informed about the system operating in our defence mechanisms in the foundation of our behavioural decisions. The system operating there presents us with a choice or conclusion, and we know this conclusion as our own decision and behave accordingly. The phenomenon called consciousness in the superstructure works depending on specific acceptances and principles. For example, suppose a person sees themselves differently from other people in a negative or positive way because of some reason (money, education, power, social status, honesty, sincerity, racism, religion, nationalism, etc.) In that case, they are already accepting the place they put themselves in.

The defence mechanisms are already prejudiced from the beginning because they rely on this acceptance. They see themselves superior or inadequate and a loser. In any case, the operation of a person's ego begins with a 1-0 win or defeat, and they try to balance this. In other words, they try to eliminate the discomforting effect of their impulse by relieving themselves through keeping people in line, judging, or reproachfully achieving superiority if they can.

To prevent the ego prejudice from being operated on, a person should first comprehend that they are not superior to, or more inadequate than, anybody. A person should also remember that their physical conditions, socio-economic structures, and social statuses are passive structures and they are active, and therefore that no passive structure can represent an active structure. In other words, no matter what their statuses are, they should not forget the fact that they are human, and therefore they are an asset needing love, respect, and trust.

If we start the case with "everybody is equal" and "everybody is human like me", we are not competing with ego. The same operates in the same way in the belief mechanism in the consciousness dimension of a person. If a person considers the Creator a holy asset different from themselves, and see themselves different from him, then they begin the case defeated 1-0 and always evaluate themselves as helpless.

The system operating here is the law of cause and effect, or the law of action or reaction. A person asks themselves the question, "If every reason has a result and I am here as a result, what was I before this and what will I be afterward?" seeing the system operating in nature and setting forth from the fact that every effect causes a reaction. Because they cannot find the answer to this question, they find themselves ignorant and inadequate right from the start. They try to complete and make sense of themselves with their inadequate feeling and cognizance and need to take refuge in the force that created them and be looked after by them. A reality under an understanding of God, through whom people will believe in themselves, originates from here.

However, if they comprehend the fact that they are a human, being human cannot be inadequacy, and they will not be at fault for being human, they will also comprehend the fact they are a part of the creator structure, and there is a bond of love between them and the Creator instead of considering the Creator as an authoritarian power. A person will succeed in being the person that they should be by becoming free. They will see that the way they can make their short life valuable and meaningful is through peace and love. They will learn to be themselves and behave in a way that is suitable for them. If a person cannot be as themselves, they may either consider themselves lacking or regard themselves as superior and different. In fact, the meaning of this is hypocrisy in any case, and this person comes to you with a different appearance which is against their own essence. Can you think that it would be a very grievous situation to live the cowardice of not being able to know how to behave towards everybody, like a chameleon, because of not being able to be themselves?

But do not be afraid. Be yourself no matter what happens. You should know that being yourself is better and more valuable than being hypocritical or being another person. Thus, you will get rid of the bother of finding a proper mask, and the fear that your actual structure will emerge one day, and people will know you properly and put you in the right place. Can you imagine that what you are eating is a hot pepper while you believe it is strawberry? This is the equivalent of your hypocrisy in people.

The system operating here is actually very simple. If you do not want to get hurt, you will not hurt another person. If you consider that you have the right to hurt someone or suppose that you cheat the other party considering yourself sly, everybody will behave to you as you behave. If this case hurts you, then you will not behave like this.

How would you feel if you had a crippled foot? Your being like this would not be your wish and choice. However, having a physical disability, although you have the right to be like everybody else, cannot be a fault or deficiency. This is because you are like everybody with your consciousness and you want everybody to see you like they see themselves. You want them to know that your disability is not a deficiency or crime. Here, everybody is able to feel like this disabled person and understand them, which gives a clue and indication of how the events should be regarded. What is important is not being sorry or pleased for not being an Olympic champion, but being able to comprehend that being a champion is not a skill.

In fact, the expectation of every person from the other party is the expectation "come to me being an 'upright' human". This does not mean to "adjust yourself according to my rights and wrongs while coming to me". What is meant can be expressed in a way that you should come as a "human" you believe in as well when you are asked what and how a "person" should be. Be sure that the humanity concerning which you call a person "human" is the same as the humanity by which I say, come being a human.

When I say come being an upright person, the thing that I want from you is not the things my selfness wants from you, but what you actually should be. What is called "me" here, is us which is formed by "you and me" and which we all say "A human should be like this." **We all know that a person should be sincere, respectful, ethical, fair and responsible.**

We can describe the easiest expression of the fact that a person's selfness should be in the right place towards other people with the integrity of the law of symmetry. If you put 100 litres of water in a 100 litre container, there will be no room in the container. Well, what else should we have put in this container that we did not put, or should we have put another thing and we did not? Yes, if we do not live alone in the world, we should also put in this container the things apart from us. If we put this person in a container, we should put justice and fairness in front of the self and selfness of a person. Because this is the necessary law of symmetry. If there is a concept or objectivity, there should be their opponent or equal. Otherwise, the meaning of existence and values is lost anyway. Now that the volume of our container is obvious, in other words, the volume and dimension of the symmetry is obvious, then there will be up to 10% space left for justice and fairness if you put your selfness and selfishness in this container at 90%. The request for energy to be in balance and neutral, or the integrity law of symmetry and the laws for the necessity to balance, the diminishing part will reveal that this will not happen in this way, and this is a problem. We perceive this problem as uneasiness, presumption or selfishness, and we form a counter-impulse.

Now that the measurement of fairness is a point of balance, in other words, it is the principle of the symmetry being half and half, what is ideal is one half is your selfness and selfishness, and the other half is justice and fairness. This is the fact that how you need something, the other party can need it as well.

Existence of fairness means maintaining the balance and the existence of justice, equality, freedom and brotherhood. This should be the basic expectation of humanity. This is because there is no other humanistic way of the energy balance of the operating system.

Let's examine why it should be like this and try to understand it. First, we should decide whether we are human or something else. If we consider ourselves as human, then we should mandatorily think as human and are obliged to be human.

For example, there is a carrion in the African savannah which hyenas can smell. They run towards the carrion; however, this carrion is not big enough to suffice the flock and only has limited meat. Well, what would you expect?

Would you expect the hyenas to control themselves, reconsider and say, "There could be creatures in this flock that are hungrier than me, and therefore it will be more suitable for them to eat this carrion first?" Or, will the hyenas be of the opinion that "I should hurry up and reach the carrion before the other hyenas so I can eat the carrion?" Or, would you expect them to say, "I will not eat it, and I will wait for you," if a hyena managed to reach the carrion before any others, in spite of their effort to reach the carrion first? Or, would you expect them to think, "Anyway, if others can manage, they would have reached it earlier and what I am doing is normal – I did the same thing they would do?"

In the case that other hyenas reach the carrion, would you like the hyenas to console themselves thinking, "Anyway, other hyenas were thinking like me, and the majority of other hyenas did not reach it like me? Therefore, there is no situation to be sorry about."

As you will see, hyenas cannot make such reasoning and do what their nature requires. Only a human being thinks of these combinations and acts "AS IF THEY ARE NOT LIKE THIS" according to the conditions. This case is the insincerity and HYPOCRISY of humans. This is because there is a perception in people's minds that experiencing and thinking of these are as if they were not usual.

However, we can think of all of them but may not live them and can behave honestly. In other words, we can say that I thought in this way and did not find it right, and we can show this courage. **If there is a bad probability about an event, and we think of it, this is not a crime or fault. The problem is when we consider what we think is a fault, we deny it, and we are not sincere.**

In fact, even if you deny something or not, you cannot deliberately decide what you will think. This is because your hardware thinks according to your principles and makes decisions. Therefore, you should apply the correct software to your hardware, so your hardware can think properly and not have to think of the things that you deem faulty.

Because hyenas behave in their nature, we call them "animals" as if they were less valuable than us. Well, if we are human, then what is the nature of "human beings"? Now that a person can think and reason, what should they do, and how should they behave?

If there are two options as right and wrong, and we understand and know this, then why do we not prefer the option that is right.

Now, this is the meaning of being human. If we cannot find a difference between right and wrong, or deliberately select the wrong instead of the right, although we understand the difference, then what is the difference between the hyena and us?

So it means that you should comprehend that you should behave like a human to be able to say, "I am human." Just because of this reason, if you deem it a skill to be a hyena or human whenever you like, you deceive yourself, and you do not know what it means to be human.

If you are human, you should act like a human and not bother with the option of being a hyena. If your benefits require you to be a hyena, and you become hyena, then you should not assert that you are human.

If someone is treating you like a hyena, then you should not take offence at it. You will both behave hypocritically and want people to treat you like a human! Well, sorry about that, but who are you? Are you the smartest and cleverest person in this world who supposes you are deceiving everybody?

Guys, as can be seen, we will come to the same point. No need for all these manoeuvres. Be human and be yourself. If you are fair and sincere, there is no need for anything else and everything will be as required.

When selfishness and manoeuvres are removed, they will be replaced with fairness and sincerity, and everything will get better and become as required.

Another operation of ego is taking advantage of opportunities. It is the operation of assertions for which no courage can be shown in the usual time by finding or creating an occasion. It is keeping an issue that you were uncomfortable with three months ago, and when you get into a suitable environment, eliminating your discomfort by using that environment as an excuse. In general, this opportunity is taken at the moments they go beyond their purposes or limits.

For example, if a friend of yours who has influence over you plays a joke on you out in public, they would either show courage, assuming that everybody will either be happy or try to offend you. You do not want to deal with this joke in any case, but if your friend feels close to you and takes the liberty, you keep quiet not to hurt them or think that you are being tested with yourself, or you consider it as presumption and keep quiet not to deal with them.

Here, being able to keep quiet is your ego's calibration settings. Your silence here is not your helplessness, but your virtue. If you need to make this person know their place, doing it preferring the way that suits you and without trying the same presumption, is the thing that defines the difference between you and that person. Selecting a suitable wording to make a person know their place is not your deficiency. Quite the contrary, it is the indication of you being a proper person.

If you use this event as an excuse for hurting your friend or exhibiting your ego, you actually do not have the intention to be a proper person. This is because, for people who do not need to be a proper person, these types of software will have no meaning.

Another most common operation in ego prejudice is the provision based on the acceptance that "you cannot understand me, you cannot understand me even if I explain". This person either considers themselves clever to an incomprehensible extent or they do not regard the capacity of the other party as adequate.

In any case, this is acceptance based on the mistake that there is an unattainable difference between one person and the other party. The majority of humanity forms these wrong acceptances, maybe without noticing it.

The only value that all these acceptances, prejudices, and all egos cannot exceed is the principle of fairness. This is because fairness is the most basic and well-supported operation covering both active and passive structures.

THE PRINCIPLES OF HARDWARE AND SOFTWARE IN HUMAN BEHAVIOURS

There is a so-called software package in living creatures that determines characteristic structure and behaviour models and enables their operation starting from the DNA. For example, this is an operation called a software package that determines how a mouse will be formed and how it will behave. Scientific studies on this issue are continuing and every day we increase our knowledge by discovering new things.

This software is more straightforward and clearer in animals and plants. However, when humans are involved, the issue becomes more complicated. This is because a person can themselves make software for their own hardware, and we write this software, updating them as long as we live.

Whatever happens, is caused by what we write, and the issue becomes more complex. As what people experience and the conditions they live in are different, results vary. The common impulses of all living creatures are nutrition, reproduction, and shelter (safekeeping). What we write in our own hardware is software about the control of these basic impulses.

However, the existence of diversity while doing these, and the differences between the diversified things, and therefore this difference (the law of symmetry), causes our satisfaction levels to differ. To balance between these satisfaction levels, the availability of our psychological defence mechanisms which exist due to our being mindful makes us different from other creatures.

The way these mechanisms work is a topic too long to explain here and has thousands of variables and combinations that are the fundamental issues of chemistry, biology, psychology, and neurology. However, we will draw attention to specific operations with reference to this superior software of people who are on the standard basis that is to be accepted as normal.

In animal and plant species, female and male behaviour models are obvious according to their different types, and there are a limited number of exceptions for this issue. Because these living creatures cannot make superior software or they make this software very slowly, their behaviours operate so regularly, they are almost non-existent.

Concerning people, there is a software package in mother and father role models. However, people can go out of existing software packages in different conditions, and the existence of thousands of negative mother and father models is an example for this.

Here, our passive consciousness becomes involved, and a person will have the consciousness and ability to select what is suitable for them no matter what their software package. In other words, if you ask a question about how a mother should be, the answer you will get is the model of an ideal mother that represents all humanity and to which nobody can object. However, if we are to evaluate each mother according to their own condition, you will be faced with the expectation (moral and other expectations) to act according to the ideal mother model even though the conditions are not suitable. In other words, you expect the "mother" to write and live her own software in accordance with this ideal mother model.

However, this is not usually a realistic approach. This is because what you want to do is the mistake, it is even the imposition of performing the passive model to each person actively. For example, how can a woman whose husband has died, is alone with her children, and has no economic opportunities, be a mother to her children according to the "ideal motherhood" model? The mother in question cannot take care of her children adequately because she will be obliged to work more.

Similarly, the answer of how a proper person should be will amount to the same thing. While each person lives their own reality, they will make the comparison of how suitable they behave to the ideal structure targeted. Here the ideal targets, for which comparisons are made, are doctrines and are passive values that make us human and whose origin is based on the active form.

- If a person can write this passive, ideal structure to their own reality,
- if they can select behaviours in accordance with this structure as a lifestyle,
- if they find it precious and valuable to act in accordance with these values,
- if they get satisfaction to the extent they act accordingly,
- then they will begin to write their hardware according to this passive structure.

Moral doctrines are intended for performing this. Even though the goal has good intentions, they will feel the void inside because their role models will have collapsed at the moment they come to understand as justification causality of this is not right. In other words, the ideal behaviour models that are based on wrong justifications will become disreputable with the collapse of reasons. If a person supposes that being ethical originates from the belief in God, they will make the mistake that there is no reason to be ethical anymore and also lose their moral values when they lose their belief. **Because of this important reason, correctly informing people and having consistency in reason is an indispensable responsibility.**

The first principle for what people's most appropriate software preference should be is that the software in question has a scientific basis. This is because science is the common language of humanity, and it is the most realistic doctrine. Science is universal, just as mathematics, music, literature, medicine, and art are, and is the real essence of the common operation of humanity. The second principle is that every person is the same (they have the same operation structure). For example, this is the fact that the other party does not want something that you do not want to be done to you, done to them – or what you like and what makes you happy will also make the other party so.

These values require love, respect, sincerity, and fairness in order to be brought to the fore. These are the principles that you need to write on your hardware for you to be a proper person. Looking after fairness, being sincere in behaviours and intentions, loving, understanding, and respecting the other party instead of hurting them, must be the leading principles.

The basic principle for which the perfect human being says "control your deeds, tongue, and desires" is based on this reality. If you write this to your own hardware as principle and doctrine, the defence mechanisms of your software package will take this as reference and command and become synchronised to each other. If you say that you will become sly, deceive people, and act as others would like, and people then do not understand this and honour you, you should know that you cannot deceive anybody except yourself, and you should not think that you have deceived them, even though they do not react to you. They must have understood you (or they will understand you in time), but they must have not responded to you. You continue to deceive yourself with the lie that you are clever and prestigious in this mistake. "Why are people insincere?" is an understandable question. However, "Why do people condescend and deceive themselves?" needs to be explained.

People's need and condescension for such insincerity is not a very consistent situation. As a result, we are all human, and we know that none of us are different from any other human. Furthermore, all of these things are not necessary. We should love people in their worst and most helpless states. This is because we will also have bad experiences, the same as everybody else, at some point. These are not weaknesses or crimes (of course, I do not mean shameful and unethical things with bad experiences). What people can call bad are humanistic things such as neediness, despair, poverty, etc. If people are experiencing these today, these people should not be the ones embarrassed, but the insincere and irresponsible people who caused these people to be in these situations. And therefore, being successful and powerful does not mean being full and being happy alone. This is us being full and happy with all of our neighbours as humans, and even with the world in the long term, as well as our ability to live peacefully with the fact that we are all brothers and sisters. The basis of the morality phenomenon is the prevention of people doing themselves harm. This is software for the prevention of bad behaviour models that everybody cannot accept. Similarly, when we ask all of humanity, they are their values which everybody accepts or does not. In other words, they are the integrity of values formed and determined by the incompatibility of good and bad concepts in the two sides of symmetry. These values are the passive ideal behaviour values every person uses as reference while reacting to the reality of their conditions. The explanations of beliefs that God commanded us to obey these values are not correct, and these values are common sense and common conscientious values of humanity.

These values are the structures of universal laws and the universal consciousness operating in us. For example, the seed of a flower is not a seed made in the garden laboratory of God and planted on Earth. The consciousness of this seed is already in its own software and written by the consciousness of the universe again. There is no consciousness other than the universe's own formation consciousness.

If what is sought is a creator God-consciousness, this consciousness is already in and throughout the universe. If a human being was aimed to be created 14 billion years after the Big Bang in the formation of the consciousness of the universe, and if humanity exists today, none of us would know it, and we cannot say this was designed this way. However, no matter how we came into existence, we are here as a result, and our existence was not a formation made in a laboratory.

Our existence is the production of specific processes and formations formed over and over with consciousness and the laws of the universe in the evolutionary process of the universe. Under these circumstances, seeking a consciousness outside the universe, referring all of these causalities to it, and attributing the answer of each question to that consciousness is an unrealistic yet easy understanding. Our own active and passive consciousness is already a part of the consciousness of the universe and even itself.

I will ask you some questions to better understand how the system operates in hardware and software issues and what the big picture is. We will enable everybody to go on a loneliness island to respond to these questions- where you will need to sincerely respond to these questions inside you.

First of all, can you tell yourself a lie within the period you will be on this island? For example, does a person need to tell a lie to themselves on a deserted island for any reason, or is it possible for you to deceive yourself on that deserted island? Even if there are no people to tell a lie to and deceive, can your hardware make you tell a lie, or can you make your hardware tell a lie on that deserted island?

Well, do you think that you will have the right to tell a lie in the case that someone is on that island, or will you say that if these people tell me lies, I will tell lies to them as well? Is the fact that you know that what you say is a lie is a secret only you know about? If you have the ability to lie to yourself, will your hardware consciousness or the consciousness you know as "me" have told this lie? Do you think it is possible for a person to tell a lie to themselves without a second person? If telling lies means a person knowing a fact and hiding it from another person, what is the extent of determining what we have the right to hide? If you cannot find something that requires you to tell lies, I wonder what the things that require you to lie to people today are?

Well, can you dream on that island?

Or, what is the difference between dreaming and telling lies?

Or, is it a lie for you to explain your dreams as if they were real?

Why do you not actually perceive the dreams you explain as if they were real?

Do you feel responsible or not according to your opinion, depending on whether your dream may come true or not?

Well, what do you think about your belief in a dream that has no possibility of coming true, but you still believe that it can?

Is it deceiving yourself what you would like to do, or is it your dream that you try to make yourself believe in?

Well, when another person tells you their dreams as if they were real, as you do, do you understand whether it is real or not?

Which references would you like to use to test and confirm what has been explained?

Do you still use the same references while explaining your own dreams?

Do you believe in something without testing what somebody says?

Would you like the dreams you say to be accepted without being tested?

Well, why do you expect the other party to do some things while you do not do them?

While you do not want to be told lies or for others to try to deceive you, why do you think that you have the right to do the same things to others?

Why do you consider the things others do to you important, and object to them while the mistakes you make are unimportant for you?

Even though you do not know what the exact responses to these questions are, your hardware knows the responses to all of them, and they will give you the necessary responses when you need them. Maybe the responses to be given will be ethical and fair or selfish and arbitrary. Well, do you not want your hardware to make you do the right thing, in any case, or would you not say that you will do the right thing whatever the conditions are?

In the case that you want this, the answer to what you should do is an issue for your software. Starting from it, I can ask you a thousand similar questions. Although there are thousands of topics and questions, the basic question they all gather and combine is the question, **"why are all these manoeuvres necessary?"**

If we get to the responses to the questions and why these responses are given, we can form a thousand counter-arguments and contrary answers, as is required by the law of symmetry. We are faced with thousands of cause and effect relationships and active and passive elements. How to behave in any event and what responses we should give are fast operating systems. Our consciousness cannot control or follow these systems. What will make these systems determined and consistent are the rights and acceptances you selected as principles. In other words, they are the principles that determine the area of movement and the neighbourhood of your hardware structure, no matter what the option is. For example, if you internalise the principle that "telling lies is not right," your hardware will work to tell the truth, even if the situation is against you. If you have multiple and inconsistent references, your behaviours will be inconsistent in the same way. You can think that there may be an option to lie, and you may have to tell lies. When you welcome the idea that "I can tell lies", your hardware takes all of these conditions as a reason for you to lie, and you lose control.

Well, is there not reasonable grounds to tell lies? Yes, there is. The answer to how we can understand what this reasonable ground is, will again come from the **fairness** principle. For example, imagine that a blood shedder, namely a murderer, is seeking out your enemy. When this person asks you whether you know where your enemy is, will you tell where your enemy is, to tell the truth; or when the same murderer asks you for an innocent person, instead of your enemy, will you tell the truth of the location of that innocent person, or will you tell a lie this time?

If you operate in the principle of fairness, you need to tell the murderer lies. If you attempt to make use of an opportunity, you behave selfishly and you tell the place of this enemy to get rid of them.

Here, the difference between having principles or not is that clear. If you are a proper person with principles, you would not tell the location of the person, even if they are your enemy and you settle an account. However, if you deem yourself sly and want to take advantage of this and get rid of your enemy, you would be wrong if you suppose you hid your real intention, putting forward the justification that you had to tell the location of your enemy. Although you defend yourself, the people's conscience hardware will know what you would like to do. Similarly, you would already know what you are doing is not right.

If you try to schedule how you would behave in a situation, you will make mistakes. The programs and calculations you make in your favour will, in the end, collapse. This is because, since the system operates with an excessive load, it will begin to act in an uncontrolled way and exhibit bad behaviours that will decode the program you have made.

Therefore, there is no need for all of this. To operate correctly, the system should work in a natural and principled way, and it should not be overloaded. In other words, the principle that "**there is no need to manoeuvre**" should be formed and settled.

The only valid and ideal principle that will perform this is the principle of "**fairness**". All of the principles of sincerity, honesty, responsibility, and justice that make a human an upright person will be resolved with the principle of fairness. In short, what is important is saying, "There should be "**fairness**" in whatever you experience or want in life, and whatever happens and whatever is experienced."

You should not wish fairness only for yourself but for all people. When you try to perform this, your hardware will start to work properly. At the end of this operation, you will automatically be a proper person. When fairness gets involved, the system will work naturally because you won't have an extra energy load. This is because the principle of "**fairness**" will eliminate the energy you spend on all of these unnecessary manoeuvres. In the case that fairness dominates in your consciousness, you cannot tell lies, or you only tell lies really out of fairness. You cannot cheat others because you become as if you were cheated. You cannot marginalise people because there will be no person to call "other". If you consider fairness based on others' behaviours to you and you behave in this way, this situation is not behaving in accordance with fairness, but making fairness a shield for yourself and using it as such. If these people lower themselves by doing this, it means they did not understand and comprehend fairness.

If we return to the big picture, we comprehend that every person lives on their own lonely islet. If the aim here is to occupy other's islets and wipe out those living there, we will always be alone, and someone will try to occupy our islet. However, if our aim is to combine these islands and form a "**continent**", we will find richness and happiness in life. When we comprehend that in the big picture, all other islets are like ours, our test of humanity will end. If a diploma is given, then we will deserve the diploma for humanity.

EXAMPLES OF THE SYSTEMS OPERATING IN IDEAS AND RELATIONSHIPS

While perceiving life, we should know that many phenomena are enabled, and as a result, what we feel at the "MOMENT" is the consciousness of that "MOMENT" when all of these phenomena are crossing at the same point.

For example, we have a history of life experiences and background considering our age, and we established the cause and effect relationship about life in our experiences. In other words, we know more or less what kind of a result we will get in the way we behave, and at the same time, we have a memory that is in our memories and of our past life experiences. All of this is data for us. This data is like filters for the similar events we experience, and they are shortcuts for our thoughts. Another source of data is the environment we live in at the moment, and our long or short-term conditions, expectations, and aims.

Another piece of our data is our biochemical structure as of the moment. They are our body chemicals such as hunger, thirst, adrenalin, fear, etc. and the conditions forming them. Another source of data is the conditions in our outer world that are independent of us. For example, these are factors such as weather, warmth, coldness, air pollution, etc.

Another data source is the potential operation for the brain, which combines, analyses, and makes sense of all these conditions, and this is our outer consciousness (passive consciousness); in other words, our creative consciousness that compares or calibrates this sense-making.

All of these intersect at the same "MOMENT", reflecting on our cognizance, and we feel a life awareness in the consciousness which we call "me". A change in this data is what changes the consciousness we feel. If we are thirsty and we realise that the thing in the glass is not water while we are taking the glass and drinking the water with our consciousness of drinking a glass of water, we stop drinking, which is the system operating very fast. We do not have the speed of perception that can keep up with the speed of this operation. If there is a difference between our intention we try to realise and the result we encounter, the time elapsing until we understand this difference is in the "moment" level, which is perhaps in the level of "hundreds" or "thousands" level of the second.

Comprehending and following this system that works close to the speed of light on a consciousness basis is nearly impossible. Therefore, we grasp and comprehend the results. However, this does not mean that this operation is random and we have no intervention.

In fact, this operation works as a computer software package, and while the infrastructure software of the hardware works, it operates in a synchronous way with the concepts of belief, good, bad, right, and wrong, which we add afterward. The law of symmetry works as a sinusoid in this operation. For example, you can imagine this as a wavelength working in the range of -1 and +1 in the coordinate system instead of a stable structure. This corresponds to the place of an event at the point of (-1) that we call the worst, and the part we call (+1) corresponds to the place we call the best. If we divide good and bad by a 100-point (-50 and +50) scale, the area between -1 and +1 corresponds to 100 points.

The neutral line we call the exact centre of the two, is the coordinate line; in other words, zero point (symmetry point or plane) and our fairness balance point. It means a narrower wavelength of a questioning or virtuous person; in other words, their getting close to the coordinate plane (neutral line). This is because a reduced wavelength means the search for narrowing this area and doing the more reasonable thing instead of thinking and living the events in their endpoints.

For example, you go to the market and ask your friend whether they have a request. Your friend tells you to buy them an "x" brand soft drink, but you do not find an "x" brand soft drink. Buying a "y" brand soft drink is your real rather than a linear thinking indication; in other words, your narrowing. If you thought in a lineal way, you would not have bought (-1) the soft drink because "x" brand soft drink was not available in the market. However, your reasoning that the purpose in your friend's requesting a specific soft drink is not the request of the brand "x", but the soft drink as a drink, thus, you think about the essence of the case rather than aspect that what is seen or requested, means that you narrow the wave area of the event. Narrowing this wavelength is an area that also corresponds to being conditioned, people's taboos, or their accepted or taught helplessness. In other words, they are shortcuts.

The healthy structure of this operation is not possible with "its operation in its accepted or conditioned state" but with being open to all possibilities of an event and determining the behavioural area that can be reasonable.

The only condition of enabling this is the principle of thinking **fairly**, looking from both sides of the symmetry of a case and being close to the centre.

This case also requires looking at the event from the perspective of the person who committed the crime instead of looking at the event from a linear thinking perspective where we can prejudge when a person commits a crime.

This also requires considering the person's conditions and their justification. Otherwise, there will be an extrajudicial execution, and it means not looking after **fairness**. This is because questioning the will of a person who committed a crime due to a pathological reason, and for what reason an aggrieved person is aggrieved, are subjects that are equally delicate in terms of fairness. Most of the time, this situation continues until the person cannot face or deal with it. After all, when pathology is involved, it means the operating systems are not operating correctly, and both the person who committed the crime and the person who dealt with the crime are aggrieved in any case. Since pathological cases are events that operate outside the system, we cannot explain them from the system, and we cannot foresee its operation.

Therefore, what we explain is an operation about the normal operation. Sometimes things become very complex and the end points of the law of symmetry and the active-passive module work together. This can be challenging for the controls and decisions of the person.

For example, you love someone so much you want the best things to happen to them, and you hope they experience these; however, you cannot tell them to "stay" even if you love them.

This is because no matter how much you love them, you do not expect that person to stay because you tell them to stay, but to stay with their free will and their own wish.

However, the person in front of you is the one on whom all doors are closed and who expects you, as the final door, to say "stay."

You cannot know this and say "stay." This person may have seen you as the final door, and they went away thinking that you did not want them, so you did not tell them to stay. They cannot plead for you to tell them to stay, or it cannot be right for you to ask them to stay although you do not want to.

As a result, there is a situation in which every person is aggrieved.

Or, in another possibility, you can enable this person to stay, telling them to stay. If this person is staying, you cannot know why they are staying, and maybe this person may go if you do not tell them to stay – these options remain of their free will. While you feel in debt and guilty because this person stayed because you told them to, the other party will make self-sacrifice, and although this person will not freely choose you, they chose you because you told them to stay and were aggrieved in some way. Another possibility is that you may have told them to stay irrespective of their freely staying and they must have stayed freely, or because you wanted.

What seems very sensitive and complex here is actually very easy. It is only one of the hundreds of mistakes we make. Every understanding here is the end point to symmetry. However, it is the involvement of active and passive sorting in the decision stage.

What is active for us is our internal consciousness; in other words, our physical consciousness (feelings), while what is passive for us is our external consciousness (belief, expectation, wishes, and dreams – or the creator consciousness, etc.). In other words, it is our decision-making consciousness or mistakes about what is right for the other party. If we consider from this perspective, our active structure (physical consciousness, our feelings) is always real and realistic. The passive structure is a probable structure, and it is generally unrealistic. When we adapt this active-passive form to our relationships, what is real for us is what we feel and want to do. What is passive is an estimation or expectation of what is right for the other party. Similarly, what is active for the other party is what they feel and what they want to do.

A passive structure for the other party is the person's own expectation of what will be right for us rather than what he will feel about us.

When both people take their own activeness as a reference, the solution to the event will be the most ideal solution. Whatever happens, the relationship will be clear, and no improper expectations will occur.

When you attempt to assign the passive structure as active, there will be a problem in any case, and the operation will be destroyed (assignation without internalisation). This is because you cannot know the active structure and the consciousness of the other party with your passive consciousness, and you cannot have the chance to know this. Therefore, your inference that the other party thinks like you will be wrong.

Yes, even though the passive consciousness of both of you and for what you say, "This is right," are common, this attachment is meaningless if the active structure is different from this. In other words, you watching the same film in the same cinema as someone else does not mean that you feel the same things. It means you wish the best for the other party, but you cannot love them emotionally.

Therefore, our passive consciousness is our ideas on what reasoning, assumption, or rights should be, but our active consciousness is our cold facts.

These cannot be exactly the same, and this is the foundation of the thing we call disappointment. Therefore, we should first be ourselves. However, to be ourselves, we should never give up and ignore sincerity, respect and responsibility principles.

We should be ourselves on condition that we maintain these principles. To do otherwise will mean everybody does whatever they want, which may cause chaos and disorder.

In fact, the same system operates most of the time in our life experiences or in all events we never question without us being aware of them. There is the mistake of this operation in our belief foundation and in the foundation of wrong opinions of people that events that are impossible in many issues, can be possible. The mistake that passive consciousness sees themselves as active, or the mistakes of the operation from passive to active, or the passive structure defining the active structure according to themselves are the reasons for many things to be misunderstood. I would like to call attention to this operation again based on an example we know.

Your mother is the source of your existence and consciousness and the person who gave you life from her body. If you believe in a God and see him as the Creator and owner of everything, you should first know that who gave you this belief in God is your mother. This is because she is the person you owe the formation of your existence and consciousness to. You cannot ignore your mother and think as if you came into existence on your own, and that your belief in God is a belief that came into being by itself in an instant. Otherwise, God did not create you directly and send your consciousness in an instant. If your consciousness omits the fact that it is passive and tries to assign itself to an active position, you will come to a forced and unrealistic conclusion such as

> "God created your mother, not for her existence, but just to give birth to you,"
>
> or, "Your mother was created by God just because she had to give birth to you"

– and you come to a conclusion that all the universe and everything created was brought into existence just for you to exist.

In fact, it means your effort to define everything except you in accordance with your own existence. In other words, it is a passive structure's enthusiasm and mistake of defining the active structure according to itself. It means your passive consciousness' assigning itself as active by omitting how your active, physical asset is formed. This case is just like a drop of water that falls by breaking off the water accumulation on the roof, by disregarding the resource it comes from and seeing itself as if it was an ocean. This mistake is the attempt of a reverse operation of the active-passive operation. This analysis separates symmetry and ignores the other half.

You cannot determine an asset without consciousness, or consciousness without an asset, and you cannot separate them from each other. None of the events like reincarnation and time travel are possible according to this operation. When we take it on the basis of belief and thought, one of them is rationalism, and the other is imaginariness. In other words, one is science, and the other is superstition, which means one is reality and realism, the other is imagination and imaginariness.

7

UPON LOVE

Love feels like a very familiar feeling to us, but when we are asked to define love, all of us are instantly astonished and need to think. All of us know the feeling of love, but when we attempt to define it, we can define it only by our feelings. The reason for this is that it is actually an active-passive operation; in other words, is it a combination of what we feel in our heart as a bodily feeling and the meaning that our consciousness assigns to love. In other words, if we separate the feeling that we have as love as body and consciousness, their origins are different; however, many of us are not aware of this separation.

We think love is a concept on its own, as many other feelings are. However, love is a combination of feelings that has a connection with almost all of our other feelings and includes many phenomena such as compassion, loyalty, respect, merit, morals, sincerity, and honesty.

Love has two main origins:, one of them is based on commitment while the other is based on innocence. The origin of commitment is based on our body, and the origin of innocence is based on our consciousness. Therefore, we find the babies of all living creatures lovely, and love them for their innocence. The technical infrastructure and operation of love has a really perfect algorithm. I will not go into its technique, but I will still write some things on the basis of commitment and innocence.

Love's origin of commitment is the desire of a part to stick to the whole. On the other hand, the fact that the part breaks off and moves away from the whole, and the part longs for, and has the perception of joining the whole, lies behind the love's origin of innocence. One of them has the desire to stick, and the other has the desire to join. Light starts to move away from the sun as soon as it breaks off, and its longing for the sun because of remaining separated from it increases as it moves further and further away. If we look at the origin of innocence through this example, from the moment we are born, we are ageing and moving away from our innocence, becoming impure, and our longing for innocence increases.

This is also the origin of our longing for our childhood. The desire for commitment involves the desire to never break off or never become separated. In other words, the origin of love is an operation that we do not want to break off from and where the desire to come back together emerges if we do break off, or it is the perception that emerges when the parts of symmetry come back together, or the energy is balanced.

This is valid for every formation in the universe. The main struggle of all formations in the universe is the desire of the symmetrical parts to come together and form a whole. Every formation desires to find a balance and become whole. The desire in our consciousness and heart (hardware) is also moving in this direction. The important part is to be able to see that the entirety of humanity is actually trying to do the same and to be able to live according to this fact.

What we call good-bad is an energy fluctuation, and what is important here is to be able to minimise this fluctuation. For our consciousness to cope with this fluctuation, our heart should be full of love because the active structure is our body and heart. Our consciousness is a passive structure. The fact that our consciousness writes good and nice things as principles on our hardware will reflect as love upon us. I do not think defining love will be all that meaningful and realistic. This is because love is a personal combination of concepts with a relative dimension and perception of feeling.

Like other operations, the operation of love also includes many factors. The operation of love in humans is directly proportional to human consciousness and expectation. People become satisfied and feel love as much as their expectations are met.

People will set the bar in a wide range, thus, the level and depth of love include many variables and parameters. Although the feeling of love originally belongs to our hardware structure, the layers of love are directly related to our consciousness. In other words, our depth of love is closely related to our depth of consciousness.

Therefore, Mevlânâ (Rûmî), who we think reached the top of love, answered those who asked what love is, with, "**be me and know, be me and know**". For instance, every person lives love at their own depth, and thus, the depth of love has no limit. When a needle pricks your hand, you know its limits of pain, but not even you can know the limits of your love. Therefore, defining or generalising love is not realistic.

There will always be someone who will go out of the limits that you define and will experience things that you cannot define. However, I would still like to say a few things about love. To be more precise, I would like to make a few definitions about the understanding of love that people think of as love, not about what love is.

The love of Creator

I love you not because of the bribe of heaven or the fear of hell,

Not because I am the natural result of the operation of the universe,

No matter what purpose I exist for,

I love you because I came from you and you are the path for love.

The love of commitment

This is the love of family or parents. This is a love that knows no limits and conditions; or a love where someone can say, "**Wherever this road ends, I will be with you and stand by you in the end,**" to their loved ones. Everyone can say this but you cannot encounter this very frequently. This is because even if people believe that they love like this, it is mostly not so. Most people will see that this is not the truth when conditions change. Even if people believe that they are sincere in their love, deep down, they mostly want to have a choice, right, or option that "**If the road ends somewhere bad, I probably don't want to stand by you there.**" However, as they do not want to face this, most people feel so but act as if "**they do not feel like this.**"

Guaranteeing love

"**I want to love you limitlessly, but it would be better if there were some conditions.**"

In fact, all people who think themselves crafty mostly love like this but act as if "**it is not like this**". As these people think themselves smart, they are sneaky and insincere. This is because when things get worse, all things may turn into conditions where they think "it would be better if there were some conditions." Namely, guaranteeing love is actually a love that does not include sincerity and is not based on feelings.

Sincere love

"**Let it be fair, I consent to whatever happens.**"

This is a love that includes equity and freedom. However, it is not as easy as it sounds. Very few people can find this love, but the rest act **"as if it is like this".**

It is possible to increase these definitions. However, if you pay attention, it is very obvious and clear how the concepts of sincerity, fairness, justice, equity, and freedom, including love, are important and necessary in human software. If you remove them, your lives will have no meaning.

For the establishment of an "upright" man, you should write them on your heart, and what will emerge when you write them on your heart is love, peace and brotherhood.

WELL, WHAT IS LOVE?

Love is the addition of a creator bond and genius to all this love operation. In other words, a two-component algorithm's increasing to a three-component algorithm which is then being synchronised. It is the state of the algorithm we say is perfect for love to achieve flawlessness. Since attempting to define flawlessness will be foolish, some may know "love".

After writing these for love, leaving love here will be throwing the ball out of bonds. As I know this, I will make a description of love begging for your indulgence, but please do not consider it as a general description. The description of love I will make will be the description the way I understand and can explain.

Love

Love is drinking poison juice.
It is burning with the same fire as your darling.
It is the outbreak of the paradox of insane pain and insane peacefulness.
Those falling in love are the ones who are close to God even though they are not aware of it.
In fact, the more you are in love, the more you are human.
All of us should know love in this form and we only feel this.
Here, this emotion of feeling is the emotional bond of our physical consciousness with the God consciousness.
It is the symmetry agreement of existence and consciousness.
God's feeling his own consciousness in our body.
If we are the beloved, what we should do is to deserve the love of the darling.
If we are the lover, what we should do is to be able to have the love of the darling, as they deserve.
Your own physical love and the love for God are not the same things.
One is your pleasure, the other is the admiration you have for God.
If you would like to combine your physical consciousness and consciousness of the Creator,
Then you should have respect for your beloved one here as you have respect for the Creator.

Now that you are so sure of your love and you are serious,
Then show this to your beloved with all your sincerity.
If you are not a sincere person, you will not understand this love anyway.
Some may understand anyway.
Those who do not understand this give their blessing.

PAYESİZ...

WHAT IS WONDERED

For those who wonder about the end of the universe, those who wonder how the end will be, and for those who think that everything will disappear, we can say that such an option cannot exist in principle. **Because movement cannot stop (cannot be stopped), and information cannot disappear.** We cannot know what the end is and how it will be, but we know that what you call the end is actually a new beginning. This is because as the law of symmetry works on balance, the process that we think "is going toward disappearance" actually constitutes the formation process of a new beginning at the same time. In short, its symmetry increases while other things decrease, and a new movement process works to form the beginning at the point of reaching singularity. In other words, what you call as the moment of disappearance is actually the moment when a new formation is triggered. We can think of this situation as an example of the formation of the stars.

Just as hydrogen gas is compressed due to gravitation and starts a nuclear fusion at the centre of the star, perhaps we can think that what we call the end of the universe is the fact that all stars die, black holes are combined and grow, and the entire universe withdraws and creates a new Big Bang after absorbing the last part.

However we think of it, we can say that the system's own information and skills carry thousands of formation scenarios like this within itself. "**So, what do we represent in this cycle, and what is the meaning of our consciousness?**" This question is an issue that people want to know about, and all of us wonder about.

We mentioned before that there is a structural difference about the universal laws and principles. The current level of science and technology is not sufficient enough to explain the meaning of consciousness. However, it is possible to explain the meaning of consciousness over the principles, acting upon the universal laws. In other words, we can define and explain what the meaning of consciousness within the systematics of principles is (these definitions are an extraction of human consciousness' definition of the cosmos).

The consciousness of all living and nonliving things in the universe is an entangled whole (the system is connected with infinite symmetry, and thus, everything is actually entangled). As everything, living and nonliving, is entangled in this whole with a consciousness of its own, we are actually entangled parts of the consciousness of the universe; in other words, of the whole. At the same time, this consciousness is actually our consciousness of symmetry that we take reference to as a principle. For instance, it is a consciousness that we take as a reference and create the concepts of good-bad. In other words, one side of the symmetry is the consciousness of existence, and the other side is the total consciousness that also includes the universal laws and principles that we know as the creator consciousness.

Although we are always connected to this consciousness, at the same time, we are creatures that are parts of the whole. Because we are parts of the whole as creatures, our consciousness represents the consciousness of existence. As we are parts, we are not aware of the fact that we are connected to the whole. The universe (matter, energy) and consciousness are entangled in each other.

If you sum them up, you create the whole of the cosmos. The cosmos is the integrity of the creator and the created or information and consciousness. Our body and tangible existence represents the Creator, and our consciousness represents the created.

In fact, these are a whole and cannot be separated. Our consciousness will not have a meaning without our body, and our body will not have a meaning without our consciousness. In other words, there is a two-element (component) singularity**. In other words, what we call the **unity of existence** is a structure that comprises and includes everything and comprises energy (information) and consciousness. However, because there will be no meaning in singularity, there should be laws and principles of symmetry because of the obligation of this singularity to be of two components. We are its energy parts with our tangible assets. However, we are not a part of it, but a whole with it, as consciousness. This is because consciousness cannot be broken into pieces like energy, and it is a whole, and it is singular.

In fact, energy (information dimension) is whole and singular. However, because of the transformation characteristic of the energy, we define it as different structures, even though everything in the universe is the same and singular in the core energy level we call quantum. We are afraid that our consciousness will also die because our body dies. However, what we are afraid of is not the extinction of our consciousness but the extinction of our memories and feelings (I will not give details and mention its content because it is a technical issue). According to our consciousness, dying means becoming extinct. However, nothing "can be extinct from existence or can be made out of nothing".

Although this principle exists, we are scared of death because there is no emotional equivalent of this principle in our consciousness, and we cannot comprehend the meaning of this principle because understanding and knowing are phenomena based on feeling; we should understand that our consciousness does not comprehend this. If your consciousness exists today, then you did not exist out of nothing. Because you will not exist out of nothing, then you cannot be extinct while you are existing. You attribute your existence in this world to a creator and a God, or a power that made you exist. Well, when you die and become extinct from your perception, can you say that God or the power that created you will die and become extinct with you?

I seem to hear that everybody says God is immortal. Just as you believe in the immortality of God, I can say that you are immortal, too. I do not say this immortality means you will not die. Of course, all of us will die; in other words, we'll complete our lifetime process as humans and wake up to another part of consciousness. However, we will always exist not as human, but as another part of the **unity of existence**. However, the handicap here is our remembering the previous history of our own consciousness. Because we cannot remember this, we get the idea that we existed out of nothing and we will be extinct again. Well, now that I am here, I should have come out of non-existence because I cannot remember my previous history, and we will have the fear that I will go into non-existence again. However, nothing can exist out of nothing and this is an impossible case, and the most basic law. In this case, it means we come from "existence" and go to "existence" again.

Our consciousness of being a part of our physical existence is our consciousness that tries to understand and seek an answer to the question, "now that I am here, why am I here?" In other words, it is our existence consciousness that is part of the whole.

In fact, the paradox of the division of the same consciousness (due to the law of symmetry), in other words, the separation of a part and a whole, enables us to think as if we are separated from the consciousness (the whole) we call the creator consciousness. The energy level and the meaning and information intensity at this point of the paradox are at the maximum level. Our awareness of comprehending this separation point and our comprehending this is not a case that can be experienced easily (explaining this **cognizance** stage of consciousness with today's science is a very difficult case.)

Our perception level in our daily lives works on the level of one-down acceptances (the law of necessity) and here is the area we can call the autonomous area. You have no chance to interfere in the system of today's conditions.

This process that we call the evolutionary process is humanity's coming to this paradox point as **cognizance**. This evolutionary process is actually "the life of humanity". It is the table on which cards will be reshuffled for later. Do not forget that if something cannot be extinct from existence, who knows how many times we sat at this table together and how many times we left this table. I do not want you to perceive my explanation as to the heaven concept of beliefs, and I do not mean we will meet there again as humans. What I am trying to say is that just because we were together before the Big Bang, we will be together after this again, before another Big Bang. Greetings and respects to all to meet in the **World of Unity** as living and non-living creatures. . .

CONCLUSION

The understanding and the doctrine of unity of existence is an archaic doctrine that takes precedence of our beliefs. Whereas beliefs and religions attribute creation to a power that makes something out of nothing, the understanding of the unity of existence is an understanding of a rational and scientific analysis (humanity will understand this better and see that this is the reality in the future).

Looking at an event with an understanding of the Creator's transformation to creature instead of looking at it on the basis of Creator and creature is the basis of today's scientific approach. For example, neither the Creator nor the creature is apparent. This is because both are the same, and therefore, making such a separation is a mistake.

Actually, if you pay attention, this refers to a transformation, and the principle of transformation of everything is indispensable and the most fundamental principle of science (active-passive operation and process). The moment you see this fact, you will comprehend that there is no supernatural structure (the structure that is against the laws of the universe), and you will be more realistic. Trying to tamper with this fact is the worst thing possible for humanity. You should know that throughout the history of mankind, people have been abused and exploited for tampering with this fact. The understanding of God defined by beliefs is like a straitjacket worn by humanity. This is because the understanding of God attributed to beliefs does not represent the real Creator's power and its genius. Humanity will not be able to see this fact without getting rid of these and finding the true path.

Above all, you should know very well that your hardware owns the information you need. Every power existing in the universe is active in your existence, and the information of everything is present in you. This active form is not arbitrary but natural, and it depends on the laws of the universe. Getting hungry when you consume energy and regaining your energy by eating something is a normal operation. The mechanism telling you that you are hungry is not an external God, but the operation of the laws of the universe which is inside you. Your consciousness of getting hungry is the consciousness of the universe in your hardware, and this has no holy aspect (feeling admiration for the information and consciousness instead of blessing them is the most virtuous attitude that is suitable for a human being).

Making unrealistic definitions and convincing yourself of these definitions is not rationalistic and correct. In the end, humanity must consider rationalism and science as a guide. Most people living in this world strive for this to be seen as soon as possible and they strive for bringing peace and happiness to humanity. We have tried to make contributions on this point as far as we can and we hope we have been successful in making even a few contributions.

Brains that have tried to illuminate humanity throughout history have actually explained the facts they saw in their own periods and their own reality. Seeing the whole picture in today's reality will be possible through science, and we hope this will occur within a short period of time.

The meaning of William Shakespeare's "to be, or not to be" is "to know, or not to know" today. Questioning is required to be able to know and learn. Question and then believe in whatever you believe, but please get rid of the laziness of believing without questioning. Please do yourself a favour and be sincere to yourself.

Believe that everybody is aware of everything. Those who suppose themselves to be incomprehensible and sly believe that humanity is fed up with you and cannot tolerate you anymore. Here is what honest people should be sure of: they should believe that humanity will face itself in the end and see the facts, and they should never suspect this. I celebrate every person who internalises sincerity and contributes to the reality at heart, and to them, I pay my respect.

PAYESİZ...

Printed in Great Britain
by Amazon

43447668R00121